The Lazy Man's Guide To Living the Good Life

By: Mike Vestil

The Lazy Man's Guide to Living the Good Life
Copyright © 2017 by Mike Vestil

ISBN: 9781520922621

Dedication

This book is dedicated to my crazy weird, yet very supportive family.. No matter how many times I fuck up in life.. You guys have always had my back. Thank you so much.

Table of Contents

Chapter 1 (You were warned)

"I am not your fucking guru" .. I think Tony Robbins said this in some form or another. So please, when you read this don't put me on a pedestal or view me as someone that walks on water. Because I would make a shitty role model. Now that I got that off my chest, I want you to understand one thing. I AM A NORMAL HUMAN BEING. And If I can accomplish the lifestyle that I wanted, then you can too.

There is nothing separating me from you... You'll hear my story soon enough. I had no advantages starting off, I was not raised in a rich family, I had no trust fund... and I did not win the lottery.

The only difference between me and you is that I went out of my way to find mentors that had the results that I wanted... And I just took fucking action.

Oh and whoops, sorry for starting this book with such foul language... You must be appalled I apologize from the bottom of my heart. Actually not really. This book is not meant to console you and tell you that everything in your life will work out just fine if you just believe in your dreams and never give up. I'd rather voluntarily step on Lego pieces before I ever create a book with a sole purpose of "motivating you." No. That is not the goal. The goal is to help give you the cheat codes to secure the good life of health, wealth, love, and happiness as fast as possible. And for that I do not have time to be nice or worry about run on sentences or improper grammar.

I am going to be up front. I am going to tell you the things that you need to hear to start living the life that you want, and I am also going to tell you the things that you don't want to hear and you are going to most likely hate me or feel somewhat offended by the time you are done reading the first chapter.

If you already feel offended... Great! You can just stop reading here, take your receipt, go to wherever you purchased this book from and return it for a full refund. Then you can take that refund and invest it in a 900 calorie hamburger where you can mindlessly eat your problems away while in traffic driving to a boss that does not know your true worth or potential.

But if you were crazy enough to pick up this book and find yourself still reading. I like you. You're my type of crazy.

As you know, the way I write is very polarizing and upfront... Some may say rude... Gasp I had no idea... Ok maybe I do. That is because I don't want to waste your time or mine. I want you to immediately read the first chapter and know right away if this is for you or not for you. It takes a very special person to follow this journey that I embarked on early on in life. It takes drive, it takes internal motivation, and it takes a dream so big that it scares small minds with people looking at you like your crazy. But heck, they are the ones that are crazy. I mean why on earth would you spend 40 years of your life going to work and building someone else's dreams when you never gave your own dreams a chance. Absolutely nuts. If you would rather settle for indentured servitude and spiritual suicide, then this book is not for you sorry.

But if you have big dreams, goals, and aspirations... And want to live a life with the abundance of health, wealth, love, and happiness that you not only want but deep down you know you deserve, then we are going to get along just fine.

Well that's it for the rant. Now I want to welcome you to The Lazy Man's Guide to Living the Good Life.

So what the hell is The Lazy Man's Guide to Living the Good Life? Well it's simple really. We have at most 100 years to live. So our main goal is to fill it with as much health, wealth, love, and happiness as humanly possible. These are the 4 pillars of the Good Life that you need to find time to focus on growing each and every day.

This book is about showing you my journey and growth in each of the pillars so that you can save yourself time, money, and failure and just learn from my mistakes

"You Can Always Tell Who The Pioneers Are Because They Have Arrows In Their Back And Lying Face Down In The Dirt" - Anonymous

You can either go out there and figure it out on your own and end up with arrows in your back, Or you can see where I fucked up in life and just learn from my mistakes because if the arrows on my back were food then I would have enough to feed an entire third world country for decades. So learn from my mistakes damn it.

"But Mike, how can I focus on growing my health, wealth, love, and happiness and actually live the good life that you speak of when I don't have any time? I mean I have a full time job, I'm a full time student, and I have a full time girlfriend... Am I doomed to live just an average and mediocre life?"

There there my child. Your first goal then is to make a decent amount of money where you don't have to worry about this job thing.

I mean if you think about it, you spend 8 hours asleep, 8 hours at work, and 8 hours doing god knows what you do when nobody's looking. That means that you are wasting one third of your life and trading your time for money.

So what are your two options to getting a decent amount of money so you actually have time to live the good life?

There are two ways to accomplish this.

Option 1:
Every day you wake up at 6 am, you get ready, you quickly eat, you drive to work, you get stuck in traffic, you arrive to work to sit there for 8 hours a day, you come home from work, you get stuck in traffic again, you go home eat, watch TV for a couple hours, you go to bed, you wake up the next day, and repeat the exact same process for the next 40 years of your life.

Every now and then after working 50 weeks in the year busting your ass building somebody else's dream you get 2 weeks to yourself where you can fly to somewhere tropical and use sand and fruity mixed drinks as an escape so you don't have to think about the real problems that you know you should be solving but are too brain dead from working so long to take them head on. You then go back to work after spending everything you saved up for for a silly little vacation and immediately get back to reality patiently waiting for every two weeks for your paycheck to come in where you take 10% and put it in your retirement fund, 40% into paying for food and shelter, and the other 50% to buy things you don't need to impress people you don't like.

Then finally when you are 65 years old you can retire off of your pension and savings and have all the free time in the world to live the good life. Maybe buy yourself that red BMW you always wanted or take an extended trip to Europe like you always dreamed of... Happily living the rest of your life in pure bliss.

As awesome as this sounds, this is actually the hard way.

Better put, Charles Bukowski once said, "how in the hell could a man enjoy being awakened at 6:30 a.m. by an alarm clock, leap out of bed, dress, force-feed, shit, piss, brush teeth and hair, and fight traffic to get to a place where essentially you made lots of money for somebody else and were asked to be grateful for the opportunity to do so?"

Now ask yourself, with your present situation...

Are you living? Or just existing? Because if the above lifestyle sounds like yours, I need you to wake the fuck up.

You cannot live the same year 75 times in a row and call that a life. But don't worry it is not your fault. You were given this "master plan" from either your parents, your teachers, your family members, and your friends. Basically being brainwashed to believe that this was your only option.

This is the problem with this "master plan" that society has created for you. When you are young, you have all the time in the world and all the energy... but you don't have any money. When you are in your twenties or thirties, you have all the money in the world and all the energy but you have no time since you are always at work. Then finally when you are old, retired, and ready to live the good life. You have all the money in the world and all the time... But guess what? You don't have the energy you once had to enjoy it. You are just merely existing and letting life happen to you instead of for you.

Now this life sounds extremely difficult and almost depressing. So why do people keep on falling into the trap of wasting their precious life away?

It's because they don't know that there is a better way available. A lazier way.

Option 2:
And that is to generate as much wealth as possible early on, put it all in a proper investment fund that pays you passively for the rest of your life. Then use all your new found time to do whatever the hell you want to do as long as you are still working on growing the 4 pillars of the good life. Wala the lazy way.

"But Mike if I have all this time and no longer have to work, why do I still have to focus on growing the 4 pillars of the Good Life?"

Because you will end up as a fat, depressed, piece of shit that's why.

You ever see celebrities go crazy and shave their head for no reason? Or drunk drive and crash their lambo just for shits and giggles? Exactly.

So that is the Lazy man's guide to living the good life in a nutshell. After you have the income that you want coming in, your only responsibility left is to just grow as a human fucking being. Is that too much to ask for?

So now it's your choice. Would you rather choose the hard way? Or the Lazy way?

"Mike this Lazy man's guide sounds awesome and all. But it sounds a little too good to be true?"

Does it sound too good to be true? Hell yes…

But that is because the ultra-wealthy have been hiding this from you your entire life. I mean if everyone in the world would do this? Who would the large companies hire to work for them if everyone was creating wealth for themselves?

The reason why it sounds too good to be true is because society doesn't educate us or teach us this in schools.

"I don't want a nation of thinkers I want a nation of workers" - John D Rockefeller

But still I get it. It is hard to truly believe that this can happen for yourself. Heck I was the same way. I had no idea that this life I am living now was possible. I thought people that lived the amazing lifestyles just got lucky, I never really thought that this could happen to me.

And if I felt this way when starting off working to build my dream, I know for damn sure that there are people out there that also don't believe that they too could create the life they wanted by simply following the proper guidelines to wealth.

The reason why we depend on slaving away to work for a paycheck is because we don't have the income we need to survive in this economy. As much as it sucks, we need money.

But what would you do if money was no object? What is the life that you would live? What aspects of your life would you focus on? What adventures would you embark on? Who is the person that you would want to become? If money was no object, what would you spend the 86,400 seconds you have every single day on?

The only thing that matters of course: The 4 Pillars of The Good Life - Growing your health, wealth, love, and happiness.

In all honesty I really didn't want to write this book, not because I wanted to keep all of these secrets to myself but because I am a pretty lazy person. I wanted to just build a business, scale it really fast, hire a team of awesome people to help run the business, and just travel the world while getting a six pack and falling in love with everyone and everywhere I would go.

However, I need to make a fucking stand and get this information out there because no one else is taking responsibility to teach people how to effectively create something that would give them the free time to focus on the more important things in life.

So this was the reason for the birth of the book. To drop some serious knowledge bombs.

Then once you have all the time, energy, AND money in the world. You can start focusing on bettering your health so that you can live longer to enjoy it, you can grow your wealth so that money will no longer be a problem for future generations, you can work on finding love and creating strong passionate relationships, and you can go on an endless adventure for obtaining happiness and to share it with the people you care about.

This book was created so that YOU can believe that this IS possible. Not just for the filthy rich and wealthy... But for the common man or woman that at one point did not believe this was probable for themselves.

But this is what you have to understand. Wealth is only one pillar of the good life... It is not the most important one. And if you go through life believing that money is the key to happiness than you will end up very rich, but very depressed and unfulfilled.

How this book works is I will walk you through my entire journey with bettering my health, growing my wealth, finding love, and searching for happiness. If a section bores you...THEN SKIP IT. You are not forced to read everything in order.

This is my story on how I found mentors in each one of the good life pillars: health, wealth, love and happiness, and how I used their experiences, their failures, and their knowledge to speed up my own learning curve and get results.

If I can help you start focusing on growing these 4 pillars alone on a daily basis, then this book won't go to waste.

Chapter 2 (Living in a hell?)

"Many people die at twenty-five and aren't buried until they are seventy-five." - Benjamin Franklin

Someone once told me the definition of hell, it's that on the last day you have on earth, the person you became will meet the person you could have become. The question is, who is the person you will face when your time comes? Will you have accomplished everything that you have ever wanted to accomplish? Would you have seen everything you have ever wanted to see? Would you have experienced everything that you have always wanted to experience?

You see I am glad I heard this quote early on because it has influenced almost every decision I have ever made every single day of my life. My biggest fear is feeling the regret at the end of my life knowing that I did not do all that I could have done.

Just imagine the helplessness you would feel right before you are about to die, knowing that there is no do-over button with life. You can't go back in time and fix it. What's done is done. And you have to live with the choices that you make today.

At the end of the day there are two things that we cannot avoid. 1) death 2) taxes. And it is the fact that I knew I wasn't going to live forever that made me realize I had to take action today.

The average lifespan of person living in the United States is 27,375 days. If you are 25 years old, you have 18,250 days to live. If you are 50, you have 9,125 days left to live. If you are 65, you have 3,650 days left to live.

How many days do you have left before it is too late to live the life you want?

Before I bring you into my world. I need you to understand one thing. Knowing now what I just told you, you need to start valuing your fucking time. Time is the most valuable thing in the world - it's not money.

But what's messed up is people are living their life as if they have all the time in the world.

Many people spend much of their life sitting on a couch watching TV, getting their excitement and sense of adventure from the characters in the movies. But if you knew you only had 100 days left to live, would you be spending that time on the couch?

After Thanksgiving, people spend hours and hours camping outside the stores just to buy something for 10-20% off. If you knew that that was your last day on earth, would you waste your precious time waiting hours to save dollars?

You can spend money and you can make money. You can spend time, But you can NEVER get time back. You only have so many days to live.

I suggest you make the decision right now that you are going to start valuing your time.

They say the youth is wasted on the young. Well "they" are correct. Many people my age don't understand that. And it is not until they are middle age, in a poisonous marriage, fat and depressed do they realized that they fucked up.

And if you are reading this and in that position and you are thinking crap it is too late for me.. Understand that there are people out there that are in a worse position than you and would kill to be in your spot.

What do I mean by that? Well if you are 45 years old, in a poisonous relationship, fat, and depressed by the time you are reading this book and you're thinking it is too late for you... Understand that there is a 55-year-old in a poisonous relationship, fat, and depressed person out there that would kill to be 45-year-old knowing what he knows now.

So the fact that you are alive and somewhat healthy means you still have time to take action and create the lifestyle you want.

I think what separated me from all the people in my age group was that I gave myself a mental picture and made myself believe that I only had until age 30 to live. I am 22-and-a-half years old at the time of writing this book. So just imagine why I take the level of action you see me taking. I am literally forcing myself to take massive action.

I am aware of the fact that I only have so many days to live. I know the exact life I want. But more importantly, I know the exact life I DON'T want. And if I fail to achieve the life that I want by the time I am age 30 (my fake death deadline), I will still have time to fix my mistakes instead of wallowing in my depression and regret that I would have done if I had given myself till age 65 to reflect on my life choices.

After reading the book 4 Hour Work Week by Tim Ferris, I came across this concept called The Parkinson's law. This is the definition in the book "Parkinson's Law dictates that a task will swell in (perceived) importance and complexity in relation to the time allotted for its completion. It is the magic of the imminent deadline. If I give you 24 hours to complete a project, the time pressure forces you to focus on execution, and you have no choice but to do only the bare essentials."

It is like in high school when you had a paper due. If the teacher gave you 6 months to write the paper, you put it off until the last minute because you think you have all the time in the world. Then after dreadfully being reminded that you have 24 hours left until it is due, you use all your resources to get that paper done by whatever means necessary. And as if by magic, you were able to complete the assignment and get a grade that would be just as good if not better than if you would have started 6 months ago.

This is exactly what I am doing with my life right now. I am cutting out all the bullshit and giving myself an imminent deadline to accomplish all that I have ever wanted so that I can create that emotional leverage needed to take all out massive action. As crazy as this sounds, this is in fact the lazy way. Because if you get what you need to do done when you are young, you have the rest of your life to just sit back and relax.

What would you do differently if you knew you had 1000 days to live? What would you do if you had 100 days? What would you do if you had 24 hours? Treat your time like this with the Parkinson's law and I promise you you will stop focusing on the things that don't matter and start focusing on the ones that actually do.

Now as you read this book, you need to start doing the same for yourself. You need to find something inside of you that motivates you to take action. Imagine what your life would look like if you don't take immediate action towards accomplishing what it is you want? Imagine being in your rocking chair at age 80. What are the things that you would regret not doing? What would you wish you could change if you knew then what you know now? Don't just glance over this and read the next chapter until you truly feel the pain of regret. I kid you not write it down. You need to immerse yourself in the pain because if you do this exercise right, you'll realize all the regrets that you would have at age 80. But instead of being depressed and feeling helpless... You'll realize that you are not 80 years old and still have a chance to make a change in your life.

Then after you see the consequences of not taking action... I want you to start imagining the life that you would live if you did take massive action today. What would the perfect day look like? What is the house you are living in? What is the car you are driving? Who is the person you get to share this lifestyle with? What do they look like? Where are the places you would go?

Before reading the next chapter. I want you to take the time and write both timelines out. One with what would happen if you DIDN'T take massive action and just let life happen to you and the other would be what would happen if you DID take massive action into actively creating your own future.

Then use Parkinson's law and give yourself a near death deadline in the future to give you that emotional leverage you need. At the end of the day the things that motivate us are moving away from pain and towards pleasure. The only downside is most people don't know what really would motivate them until it is too late and they're too old and depressed to care. But there is still hope for you!

"How can you achieve your 10-year plan in the next 6 months?" - Peter Thiel. By Parkinson's Law and finding the motivation you need to make the decisions you need to make now instead of postponing them for later.

So take 5 to 10 minutes to write the two timelines and begin to look at them every single day as a reminder for what your life would look like if you don't take action, and what would your life look like if you did.

Just like how less than 10% of people that buy books actually make it to reading past the first chapter. Only 10% of you reading this will take the time to actually do the above exercise.

And it makes sense. When 90% of the world's wealth is controlled by 10% of the population… it's the 10% that are the action takers of the world. The only question is which one are you? Are you going to be a part of the 10% and create results or are you going to be a part of the 90% that will just create an excuse?

If you are still reading this and still not writing the two timelines... Just know that you are only hurting yourself.

Chapter 3 (My Background story)

So you want to live the good life huh? I did too. But if you are going on this journey with me you need to understand how my brain works to fully understand where I am coming from and why I am the person I am today.

"Mike you were conceived on that very billiard table right there," My dad would jokingly tell me whenever we would visit our distant family members that allowed my mom and dad to live in their basement until they both got up on their feet. Back in the early 1990's my parents had just recently immigrated to the U.S. from a small island in the Philippines. And if you know anything about this beautiful island is that the Filipino peso is literally nothing compared to the dollar. It would take about 50 Filipino pesos to equal just 1 U.S. dollar so my parents started with nothing but each other and a dream to live the American Dream.

My beautiful mother whose name is Daphne came from a family of what she calls "One day millionaires". At one point her family received a lot of money in a short amount of time due to gambling and savvy business skills. HOWEVER, as fast as the money came in, it quickly left her family's hands as they were big spenders. They became broke within a couple of years. They were "millionaires" (not monetarily but in their own right) for just one day until they spent it all on things they really didn't need. One day they had everything, the next day they had nothing. Seeing her family go through the ups and downs of business, she knew that she needed to go to the U.S. to build a life over there as the economy was very unstable from where she grew up. That is when she packed her bags and moved to find a job in the states where she can start her new stable life.

My mother is amazing. She is stubborn and at times borderline crazy, but she taught me what it means to be independent and to make my own decisions. She also was one of my first mentors as she told me ever since I was young to not make the same bad decisions her family had made when they lost all their wealth.

My dad is an interesting character. Al is a man with many talents. He had hippie glasses, worked in sales, and had hair all the way down to his butt at one point in time. He has the ability to win over anyone to liking him and I have never seen a man command an entire room with such presence. Wherever he went people looked at him with respect. It was my dad who taught me to not be afraid of taking calculated risks and that failure was all just feedback on how not to get something done. That if I failed enough, I would run out of ways on how something does not work and would start finding something that did work.

My Dad followed my Mom to the United States and made a living by selling newspapers to save up to one day become an engineer and it just so happened that around that time that I was born!

They had a difficult time creating me so my dad took these super sperm pills to make something happen, so after I was conceived on the billiard table, I was basically synthetically born which makes me a cyborg superhero - or at least I wish.

I was born in a freezing cold Midwest December in the suburbs of Chicago. I was just a bald naked baby with a head the size of an overgrown cantaloupe and was nameless for 3 days. After my dad and my grandpa was watching a Michael Jordan game, they decided to name me Michael.

My childhood was pretty normal. I was severely underweight, suffered from asthma attacks and was called booger boy by my peers. It was just a sinus infection damn it but they didn't understand. Just like a booger, once a name sticks... It sticks. Every morning I would cautiously walk to the bus stop with my oversized backpack and inhaler to watch out for the local bullies that lived in my neighborhood. Those assholes wanted my Pokémon toys and would chase me every single day and threaten to "dog pile" me if I didn't hand them over. I had no idea what a dog pile was at the time but man did that threat sound scary.

Since everyone in my neighborhood was older than me and bigger than me, I spent most of my time fighting imaginary dragons and riding around in my Harley Davidson tricycle. One of my favorite drinks at the time was Kool Aid and I would drink that as if it were water - which most likely was the reason for my annoyingly excessive high energy and childlike bounciness that has seeped into my adulthood. I noticed that my trusty tricycle had no cup holders, so I created a makeshift cup holder with duct tape, glue, and a cloth hanger. I mean do you really expect me to fend off these dragons without staying hydrated?

I had to hang up my dragon sword the moment my sister was born. Angelique came out of my mother like a tiny little alien that always tried to eat my damn balloons. Even though she started off annoying as all hell she was really my first childhood friend and I knew that I needed to become the perfect role model for her and make sure that she would always stay out of harm's way.

When people ask me "Mike what is your why? What is the reason why you want to become successful?" and even though I tell most people that my why is to live the craziest life possible that would be fit for an action-adventure-romantic-comedy movie, in truth it is the faces of these 3 amazing people, my mom, dad, and sister that flash in my mind to always keep on going no matter how hard the challenges I may face get.

When you are on your journey you need to understand that this path is much bigger than just to satisfy your own selfish needs. The decisions you make today are what affect you and the people around you, either for the better or for the worst. I know this now, but the question is do you?

Who are the people in your life that you care about?
How do they motivate you?
Who are the people in your life that you are grateful for?
Why are you grateful to have them in your life?

Begin to be aware of these people and the moment you feel like you are alone in this journey to living the good life, you will be reminded that you are not alone. That this journey you are now on is not just so you can live the Good Life, but so the people that care for you and have helped you to get to where you are can also share in the Good Life with you.

If it wasn't for understanding this, I would have given up a long long time ago. But it is these 3 people in my life that initially lit a fire under my ass to take massive action.

Chapter 4 The High School Rebel That Became A Thief

Going into high school, I really didn't know who I was. I had a handful of really close friends and would bounce back between different groups just trying to figure out my identity. One day I was the jock that played sports, the next day I was on the chess team kicking ass. One day I was focusing on playing music in a garage band, the next day I was getting drunk and running away from the cops when they would bust a party for underage drinking after I snuck into a party filled with the "popular kids" that I wasn't even invited to. I tested my identity to the limits early on. I would have a preppy haircut and would wear a polo with a pukka shell necklace one day, and a buzz cut, green contact lenses, and an eyebrow piercing look the next day.

Everyone thought I was weird but I guess my lame jokes and somewhat hilarious personality is what let these people allow me to stick around

"Why fit in when you're born to stand out" - Dr. Seuss

I guess my entire life I have always been an outsider. More like a rebel to the status quo. Deep down I just knew that I wanted to be different than everyone else. I couldn't stand to live a life where I would just fit in. And due to that and an identity struggle I stuck out like a sore thumb awkwardly living though my youth years.

The next thing I wanted on my list of testing my identity out to find out who I really was was to buy a motorcycle. But of course I had no money. So I had to hunt for a job.

My first job I applied for was for a clothing store called Pac Sun. I got hired, signed the papers and all, but they never gave me the schedule for when I should work. So technically I may be working for them still or maybe not, I have no idea because I was never updated.

The second job I applied for was to work at the movie theater. I was excited when I got the interview scheduled with them. I thought how awesome it would be to watch movies for free and eat all the snacks that the theater had to offer. But sadly I took a nap, overslept, and missed my interview. After trying to convince them for one more chance, they told me straight up that I was too lazy and would never get a job at the movie theater.

My third job I applied for was to work as a summer camp counselor. After getting hired, my typical 8-hour work day would consist of rock climbing, swimming, playing tag, and drinking gallons of chocolate milk with a bunch of 5 year olds. It was pretty awesome but I was only getting paid like $7 an hour. It took me 2 years to save up $2000 to buy the motorcycle that I wanted.

Since I was really keen in saving my money for this motorcycle, I would partake in petty theft to get the smaller things for free so I can protect my nest egg of course. I'm telling you I am really not the best role model. I would go to grocery stores, see a bag of chips, and just shove it in my pants, then I would walk out. I did this with chips, cookies, protein supplements, sunglasses, you name it I would just shove it in my pants and just walk out the door. I felt invincible... And slightly weird knowing that everything I had stolen had direct contact with my man junk. Then one day my friend Dom and I end up going to a department store and I saw a cool t shirt that I wanted. By habit, I shove it in my pants. Dom sees me, and he too gets a shirt and shoves it in his pants. We then made the dumbest decision to see who can take the most stuff and so we just start running around stuffing the most peculiar of objects down where the sun don't shine.

As I get ready to leave, I call my friend to see if he is ready to go. No answer.

So I thought that he was already outside. As I walk out the door, a large burly man the size of a baby elephant bear hugs me and it was in that moment that I thought I was going to be kidnapped. There was a smaller chubby lady next to him and I was just looking at her wondering why the hell she was letting this happen. She grabs my phone and that is when I thought the kidnapping was going to be turned into a mugging.

"Come with me now" the man demanded

We then go back into the mall. Turns out the guy was not there to kidnap me but was a "secret shopper" whose sole goal was to find people that would steal stuff and bring them to justice. He brings me into mall jail where I arrive to see my friend Dom detained on a hand railing. He looks at me and smiles.

"They got you too huh"

They made us pull everything that we had out of our pants and it was the most awkward situation ever. One by one I pulled out a t-shirt, a pair of shorts, sunglasses, a pair of socks, a candy bar and my friend did the same.

You are probably wondering how the hell I fit all that stuff in there, my secret was that I would wear really baggy sweatpants and a baggy sweater. My compression shorts I wore underneath were what kept everything fastened. I came in a skinny boy and would leave looking like a fat tub of lard.

After we were basically cavity searched he brought us to the cash register and said that we each had to pay $500 for damages to the store. My friend freaked out as he did not have that type of cash. So I ended paying $1000 that day for me and my friend to walk away without the store calling the police or telling our parents. To this day our parents still don't know... Until of course they read this far in the book and to that I have to say sorry mom and dad.

But that was half of my net worth gone. It took me 2 years to save up $2000 and only a couple of seconds to lose half. It was at that moment that I knew the value of money. How hard it was to make it, and how easy it was to lose it.

Thanks to getting caught and ending my petty theft spree, it was in that moment I knew that I needed to do something with my life that would give me an obnoxious amount of money.

Thanks to this mishap, I knew that I was going to become a dentist.

Chapter 5 The dentist that never had a chance

I honestly don't know how I did it. It may have been through sheer will, a slightly photographic memory, or the countless amount of energy drinks that I would pound to my face every night before the deadline. But I managed to convince the dental school at Marquette University to accept me into their accelerated program. Meaning I already had a spot reserved for me in dental school by the time I was 19 years old. All I had to do was do 3 years of undergrad and then bam I could start dental school and become a dentist that makes bank and saves the world one cavity at a time.

But there was only one problem, I had no idea how to pay for it. My other option before was to go to community college so that I could save up money and then worry about getting into dental school. But to everyone's disbelief, including my own, I got accepted into one of the most competitive dental programs in the nation. The only caveat was that I had to figure out a way to come up with $40,000 a year for the next 7 years to pay for the tuition.

It was too good of an opportunity to pass up so my mom ended up increasing her workload from 8 hours a day and got another job to work for a total of 16 hours a day. My dad took every single overtime shift that he could. And for the next couple of years our lives consisted of my parents working and sleeping, barely seeing each other and sacrificing everything, just so that I could have the proper college education.

Even with their hard work, I still also had to take out student loans to cover everything else. But together we believed that this "investment" was worth it because then right after college I would be able to start immediately earning 6 figures and pay back everything my parents worked so hard to give me.

The first year of college was a blur. All I remember was sleeping in the library and making sure I maintained my grades. I have Asian parents so it was either I had good grades or I was disowned from the entire family. No pressure whatsoever. I was able to maintain the requirements of the accelerated dental program and even managed to get a girlfriend somewhere around this time as well! Everything was hunky dory.

The second year was a little bit better. After successfully completing an entire year of college... I began to understand the power of the Pareto Principle.

Vilfredo Pareto was an Italian economist who observed that 80% of income in Italy was received by 20% of the Italian population. He then realized that this was the case in everything. About 20% of a certain input will result in 80% of the output. For example, like how 20% of the population were responsible for producing 80% of the wealth, 20% of the actions that you do are responsible for 80% of the results that you want. The other 80% of actions you COULD do would only account for 20% of the results. So which would you want to focus on? The 20% of actions that give you more results or the 80% of actions that give you less results? This is the secret of the Lazy Man's Guide to Living the Good Life.

You need to start cutting out the actions that you do every day that do not product 80% of the results you want. At the end of the day, for me to maintain the program requirements and get into dental school where I actually get to start learning about things that pertain to my profession instead of memorizing dumb things in school that I would have no applicable usage for in the future (like the

Pythagorean theorem or the quadratic formula), all I had to do was to score high on all my exams.

So instead of slaving away at the library and worked harder to get that result... I worked smarter by networking will all of the upper classmen that were in the program before me. I was able to get every single old exam that dated as far back as 1999-2012 for most of my classes. I then analyzed each exam for each year and notice that there was a pattern for which type of questions were asked.

I then studied for an hour or two the night before an exam solely on the recurring topics in the old exams. And I was able to score higher than all my peers that spent most of their time in the library while I was spending most of my team hanging out with friends, working on building a stronger body, and began reading books that started to change the way I would think for the better.

What are the results that you want in life?
Are you focusing on the 20% of actions that you could do to get 80% of the results you want?
Are you focusing on spending most of your time with the 20% of people that give you 80% of your happiness?

The power with the Pareto principle is that it allows you to maximize the amount of output you receive from the input that you put in. This is very important especially when you realize that our time runs out every single day. So the more we can get out of our time the better.

Combine the Pareto principle with the Parkinson's law and you will be a force to be reckon with.

How can you apply both principles in your life? How can you use it to better your health? For example, 20% of activities in the gym give you 80% of the results, if you want to build muscle then the 20% of activities you should do is compound movements using free weights NOT the treadmill. How can you use this to better your wealth? 20% of your activities that you do actually give you your wealth. For example, many business people think that staying busy and looking at emails all day will increase their revenue, but what you will learn later on in the wealth pillar section, the 20% of activities that create 80% of results are focusing on 1) creating traffic 2) capturing leads 3) converting sales. We will get more into that so don't worry. I just want you to start understanding how you can use these two principles to start changing the way you live your life so that you can have more quality experiences instead of quantity.

Chapter 6 Paging Dentist Mike Vestil?

My third year of college was a little different.

And that is when my entire life changed. I was stuck in a crossroads and I had no idea which path to take. Half of me doesn't want to write this but the other half of me knows that this is the only way to give myself the closure I need.

Okay now let's backtrack so you understand, but in all honesty I have no idea where I should even begin. Let's start with the beginning of Junior year. Everything started off just fine. I moved into a new apartment, my best friends where my roommates, and I had the most amazing girlfriend a guy could ask for. But something was very different that year. I think it started the first time I visited home after a while of not seeing my parents. When I walked into my house for the first time in a long time to see my parents, something was different. I noticed their personalities and how it seems they were just drained with life. There was no excitement, there was no joy, there was no happiness. It was as if they were just empty shells which at one point used to be filled with human emotion. They looked like they had given up.

The first time I visited shook me up pretty bad. But I ended up just going back to school and repeating my daily rituals. However, every 3 months I kept on visiting my parents and something crazy happened right before my eyes... I literally saw both of them getting older right before my eyes and it scared the shit out of me. Every single time I would come home I noticed that their hair was a little bit greyer, their laughs were a little bit shallower, and the pain that they hid behind their smiles were getting a little more obvious.

While I was in college, my parents were literally committing spiritual suicide as they spent all their time at their job and not enough time with each other. I would come home and hear them fight about money, I would see sides of them that I did not exists, and I was terrified. How could this go on for the next 4 more years of schooling? What was once a loving relationship filled with awkwardly blatant flirtatious comments between the two was now just filled with hate and blame.

This is when I started to have a little mental crisis. I started going through negative self-talk and blaming myself for the reason why my parents were fighting. Seeing my parents slowly get older every single time I went home, kind of like how you would see the pictures in a flipbook animation move.. Knowing that the pages in the book would slowly come to an end with a horrifying ending.

And just when I thought that it could not get any worse, it did. While in school, I found out that my parents were going through a house foreclosure. They were doing everything in their power to pay the bills and my tuition but they always ended up short on the house payments.

I remember one day as I walked out of class, I remember getting a call from my dad. The tone of his voice sounded defeated as if he was a dog that was trying to run away with his tail in between his legs but couldn't. I could tell that he didn't want to have this conversation. But he told me that we were again behind on the bills and that he did not have enough to pay for this month's tuition bill even after taking out more student loans... He then asked me if he could borrow $1700 from me to pay for the tuition. All I had at the time was $2000 after saving up another $1000 after paying for stealing from the mall... But after this I was down to only $300.

Every day I would hang out with friends and fake a smile. None of them knew what I was going through and I didn't want to burden them with my sob story. I didn't want to be pitied for. But the emotional baggage I felt through this tough financial times was killing me from the inside out. I started to drink excessively, I started picking fights with my best friends, and I even started to lash out and getting angry at my girlfriend - the one person that was always by my side the entire time. That year was just filled with poison... And all because I did not face the problems I needed to face head on. I hid behind alcohol, I hid by blaming others, I hid by blaming myself. Instead of doing something to fix my crappy situation I blamed the world on why everything turned out the way it turned out.

"Don't wish it was easier wish you were better. Don't wish for less problems wish for more skills. Don't wish for less challenge wish for more wisdom" - Jim Rohn

So with the money problems I was facing getting worse and worse, so did my health... I was getting a little chubby and my friends were too nice to call me out. My relationships got even shittier. Fights with my best friends were frequent and fights with my girlfriend was almost on the daily. The thing was it wasn't even their fault... It was all mine. And all the happiness I once felt... Was completely gone.

You see money can't buy happiness, but the funny thing is when you have no money... It creates a hell of a lot of problems. That year, I ended up losing my best friends, I ended up losing the love of my life, and I ended up losing confidence and belief in myself. All because I was not man enough to face my fears and take on my financial problems instead of hiding behind my excuses. But like I said... This was all my fault.

I remember after junior year was over. Everyone went back home to visit their families for the summer, I slept on the floor one day because I felt too much self-hate to allow myself the comfort of sleeping in a bed.

The apartment was quiet, the floor was cold, and I've never felt more alone in my life.

That year I also was working as a dental assistant in an office so I could start getting a head start in my profession

But as I laid on the floor...

I started imagining what dental school would be like. I would enter as one of the youngest dental students in the nation being a year ahead everyone else that very fall after the summer season.

I would be one step closer to living my "dream"

I asked myself, is dentistry really for me? I mean it was the very financial strain that caused me to ruin my relationships, my health, and my happiness... And if that is what it would do to me now I couldn't bear to witness what it would do to me in the future.

So the summer right before I would enter dental school... I left.

"It is in your moments of decision that your destiny is shaped" - Tony Robbins

I was done feeling sorry for myself and I was tired of feeling depressed and sad all time. So instead of waiting to achieve success when I became older as a distinguished dentist... I knew that my family needed results fast because my sister was about to start college soon too. I did not want the strain that existed in my family to get even worse when my sister would start to begin school as well... And I didn't want her to go through the same hardships and emotional pain as I did.

"What the hell mike, I read your blog... I thought you were a dentist you liar". To lighten up the air with this frequently asked question... Notice in my blog I say how I used to spend most of my time in the "dental field" which is what I did. I would stay in the dental office 8-12 hours a day basically being my dentist's bitch and doing her dirty work. This is also around the time that I noticed that I was not passionate about this industry and I couldn't see myself doing this for the next 40 years of my life.

"So what does this mean Mike, are you a college dropout?" When people ask me this question, still to this day I am not sure. It sounds a little confusing when I explain this but this is what I mean. So how the accelerated dental program at Marquette University works is you end up squeezing 4 years of college education into 3 years of schooling and you start dental school your fourth year of college. So I was done with all of my prerequisites and completed all my undergraduate classes that I need to graduate. However, since the dental school doesn't want their students to leave to find a cheaper dental school option (as tuition can get up as high as $60,000 a year) they don't give out the degree to the students in the accelerated dental program until after they completed at least one year of dental school. This shackles the students to the program and makes them pay their tuition instead of forfeiting that possible revenue to another college institution... Meaning I had to pay another $60,000 just to get a piece of paper to tell me how much I am worth. I did not believe that this was fair.

I never advertise publicly that I am a college dropout (even though I want to) because I do believe that college is a great tool. I am not against college. However if you want to become an entrepreneur, then I truly believe that college is not for you. But if you want to go the cliché route and become a nurse, doctor, lawyer, or engineer than of course college is a great bet.

And so my story continues... After leaving college and the dental field forever, I had to figure out what the hell I was going to do next... My health was horrible, my love life was in shambles, I was a depressed unhappy piece of shit that was broke.

It seems like the biggest thing that was preventing me from living the life I wanted was the money that I didn't have. If only, I could just find a vehicle that I could use to gain financial success faster than I would have as a dentist, then I would actually have the time to transform and grow in my health, love, and happiness.

But the hardest part was finding that new vehicle.

Chapter 7 Picking up the broken pieces

"The same hammer that shatters the glass forges the steel." - Russian proverb

The summer following was one of the hardest time periods of my life. I had no friends, lost my girlfriend of 4 years in a blink of an eye, and had no resources.

But one thing I did have was drive and hunger. I started devouring books like a fat kid does with cupcakes trying to learn as much as I could about creating wealth so that money never has to be a problem again. One of the books that changed my life was written by Tony Robbins called Awakening the Giant Within. This book was like 400 pages long but I read it within a couple of days. I was mesmerized by the stories that he would tell of people that even against all odds, would still prevail to live the lifestyle that they wanted. This was exactly what I needed. If I do recall correctly, there was even a story out there of how a guy ends up getting in a plane crash, becoming paralyzed from the waist down, suffering severe burn marks to the face and still managed to win over the hearts of the people and live the good life. It got me thinking... People that started with less than me, still managed to create something of themselves. If they can do it why can't I?

I knew right away that I needed to immerse myself more into this new world of personal development and self-improvement. I knew in order to grow my wealth, I needed to become more valuable to the marketplace in general. So in order to do that I had to turn to people with the results that I wanted so that I can imitate their beliefs, mindset, and actions so I could achieve a similar result.

That summer I managed to save up enough money to buy 4 tickets to Tony Robbins' live event that just so happened to be held down the street (and by "saving up money" I mean saving up a little and putting it on my new credit card lol). I knew that what I was going through my mom, dad, and sister were going through the same problem in one way or another. So I needed them to experience this event with me. After I bought the crazy expensive tickets I was again broke but guess what... It didn't matter because I was invested into learning. If you ever have a chance to ever go to a live seminar I definitely recommend it by the way because you will never find people who are more aligned with your goals, your dreams, and your aspirations as the people you meet in these rooms. These are people that are going through your same struggles, but instead of crying about it like I was, they are finding mentors and taking massive action into getting those issues in their lives solved.

For anyone that has never been to a Tony Robbins event, and you come in halfway through the live seminar… You will be shocked and feel as if you are crashing a cult party that just drank the magical Kool-Aid. As you enter the room, you will witness anywhere from around 5000 to 8000 people standing up on their feet or on their chairs and just screaming in joy and dancing and you will wonder if you are in the right room or not.

It was this very event that left a huge impact on my goals and shifted my focus on what I actually wanted to do with my life instead of what other people wanted me to do.

One of the most memorable moments is when he goes through an exercise of imagining what your life would look like if you don't take the actions you need to make today because you were either too afraid or not confident enough, and how those decisions have permeated and affected your entire life thereafter. I don't know how the hell he did it but as if by magic or some mystical sorcery, within seconds the entire room was screaming in terror. I will never forget the shrieks of hearing 8000 people at once express the feeling they would feel if they came to the end of their life knowing that they did not live out to their full potential. There is something about witnessing 8000 people's regret and remorse all at once that gives you something a book could never give you. It anchored in me pain. The pain I needed to be aware of that I knew I did not want in my life.

You see most people don't even know what life they want. More importantly most people don't know the life they DON'T want, so they are forced to be satisfied with whatever life gives them. If you never put in the destination for where you want to go on your GPS, how on earth can you arrive to where you want to be? Going to this event gave me the emotional push to make sure I set my GPS coordinates to where I wanted to end up in life and also made me set the coordinates of where I DIDN'T want to end up.

Before I left that 4 day event we went over our goals and on a piece of paper I had written a 12 month goal. I wrote down $10,000 a month. Sounds reasonable right? I mean that is how much a dentist makes so why not.

"Set a goal so big that you can't achieve it until you grow into the person who can" - unknown

But before I turned the page, I added an extra 0. So the goal was to create a business that made $100,000 a month in the next 12 months. Awesome. The only problem was I didn't have any business plan I could work with.

This is when the worst year of my life became the weirdest. Almost as if in that exact moment I set that goal sparked an immediate chain of events. That some may say happened by luck. But I know it was much more than just that.

But seriously, even if you don't have the money. If there ever is an event with a well distinguished speaker in your area like Tony Robbins... Do everything in your power to get there. One of the best investment I have ever made, even though I didn't have the money to actually attend.

Chapter 8 My first attempt at business

So with my new found goal of $100K/month in next 12 months. I needed to get moving, but immediately into my journey, I ended up falling prey to a network marketing company and lost a lot of money that I couldn't afford to lose... But one thing it did give me was the access to people my age that were already achieving financial success. A close friend told me that there was a guy my age that was traveling the world and making $7,000 a month. I quickly wanted to hear his story. This guy's name was Zac and he was the first person I had ever met my age that was doing something for himself instead of following the plan that society gives you. I did whatever I could do to be around this dude as I wanted his success to rub off and on to me.

Everyday I would call him to get inside his head to understand how his mind works. What decisions did he make that led him to where he is today? What beliefs did he have that I did not yet possess that allowed him to experience success earlier on than most adults? What failures did he go through so that I don't have to make the same ones? I wanted to take the blueprint that he had and apply it to my first business. I learned a lot from Zac, he was the first person that I saw face to face in person that was living the life I wanted. But now the hard part, I had to build my team of sellers.

Now in order to become successful in Network Marketing, you have to recruit a shit ton of people. For this very reason, it gets a very negative light in the media as many people believe this is a pyramid scheme where only the people at the top make money.

Regardless if you believe it is or it isn't, one thing that it taught me was how to handle rejection and failure. When I was running around trying to sign people up for this thing that I had no idea what it even was, I was called names, I was yelled at, I was laughed at, and I experience something that I had never experienced before. But something happened while failing over and over again. Subconsciously it made me sharper, it grew my confidence in myself, I developed rhino skin and could handle rejection and failure, and it instilled with me a conviction that you now hear in my voice whenever I record any videos.

I once heard a story of Michelangelo, an Italian sculptor from the renaissance. He created the Statue of David which is one of the most iconic marble statues ever created during the era. People asked him how the hell he was able to make such a masterpiece from such a crappy piece of marble. Michelangelo responded that the perfect statue was always inside the giant piece of marble, all he had to do was remove the excess pieces.

What excess pieces do you need to remove from your identity to show the badass entrepreneur that is truly inside you?
Any limiting beliefs you need to remove?
Any toxic people you need to remove?
What excuses do you need to remove?

That is exactly what happens when you go through a high volume of failure in a short amount of time. You get exposed to all of these opportunities to figure out what you need to remove from your identity. At first it is depressing and you just want to give up, but something weird happens when you keep on going. It's as if almost by luck. You end up becoming successful, by chipping away all of the excess pieces that you once had, to show the real potential inside of you that always existed. So even though I did not have success in network marketing, it did develop my entrepreneurial mindset and brainwashed me in a positive way. The reason why most people never live the life they want is because they are not willing to let themselves fail. But it is in failure when you can truly become successful.

You can calculate just how successful you will become by asking yourself how many times did you fail today? Then right after you have the list of all the failures, immediately ask yourself what did you learn from those failures? This creates a feedback loop that allows you to now see failure as just negative feedback. Then all you have to do is just review where you went wrong, change your plan, and try again. If you do this as much as you can, you will become successful because the probability of success swings in your favor since you have given yourself more attempts to actually try and succeed. You have chipped away all of the excess marble that has been preventing you from living the life you want.

Another thing that Network Marketing did for me was it surrounded me around a group of positive people that also had the same goals as I did. Before, when I was in college, I was surrounded by people who didn't want to become entrepreneurs. You become the average of the 5 people you hang around with the most, and I could tell that their lack of drive was affecting mine.

Ever notice that when a depressed person walks in a room, everyone seems to get just a tad depressed for no reason? How about when you are talking to a friend that really isn't funny at all, but whenever they tell a joke and laugh at their own joke because they think it's funny, even if the joke is not funny you still end up laughing. I have a really close friend, his nickname is Poppy and I still have no idea why that is his nickname but every single time he laughs, the people around him laugh because of just how ridiculous his laugh is, not because the joke is funny. But because he thinks it's hilarious, you also end up finding it hilarious.

Regardless if you like it or not, the people around you affect you as much as you affect them. It can either be uplifting and motivating or it can be harmful and detrimental. Look at the people you spend most of your time with... Notice any similarities between all of you? Most likely yes because as humans we learn to adapt and absorb each other's qualities since we are social creatures. But this can have a negative effect on you if you want to live good life. I am not telling you to ditch your friends (or maybe I am you will never know). What I am saying is if you want to use the Pareto principle with this one, you need to start spending your time with people that have the results you want or are on the same journey as you are if you want to reach your goals faster. That is exactly what I did.

Who are the people you spend most of your time with?
Are they positive or negative influences?
Who are the people you can start hanging around with that have the results you want?

Around this time, I met a friend of a friend of a friend that needed a place to stay. His name was Jacob. I had no idea who the hell this guy was but a close friend of mine said that he just signed up for our team so I was like what the heck sure. I go to sleep slightly afraid that I may get murdered by this random Half-Asian Half-Mexican dude that was just left at my doorstep. I wake up early the next day and walk down into my kitchen to find Jacob eating an entire fish to himself and licked the meat clean from the bone. What did I just get myself into.

Long story short we end up going to a club where I attempt to find a new girlfriend (only said half-jokingly). After getting rejected over and over again we ended up walking out with our tails in between our feet. As we got into the car for some reason, he started talking about eCommerce - the ability to sell products online through your own storefront. In my mind I had no idea if this guy was for real or high on drugs, but what he said intrigued me. He said that he knew a guy who knew a guy who knew a guy and that I should add this other Asian guy named Charlie if I wanted to try this eCommerce thing out. I don't know what propelled me to add this other random guy that Jacob was speaking of on Facebook, but I did it anyways.

After that weird night with Jacob the random stranger (who is oddly one of my closest friends right now) everything in my life almost seem to magically fall into place. The day after I added Charlie, he posted a screenshot of his eCommerce sales on his wall. This guy was only a couple hundred dollars short of making $10,000 in one day selling t-shirts... My jaw hit the ground in disbelief. He then said that he was doing a webinar training in 24 hours which I ended up signing up for after stalking all of his social media profiles to see if he was a real person or if he was just another scam.

I had no idea that you could make $10,000 online in a month much less a day, my mind was screaming too good to be true but something inside of me was curious into figuring out if this guy was for real or not. I attended the webinar and was just blown away. It was at that moment that I knew I had exactly what I needed to create the life I wanted. I found a mentor that had the results that were aligned with my goals, and I made sure that I would do whatever it takes to take all the information that was in his head and to download it into mine.

After the webinar he offered coaching to a select few individuals for $1400. Without hesitating, I immediately swiped my credit card even though I did not have the money that I needed. I was already accustomed to failure so the worst case scenario was that I would lose my money and learn a lesson which I can easily bounce back from. My first month I ended up making $5K in sales, by December of that year I did $100K in December alone, and after my first year I cleared over $2 million in sales.

Looking back, it sounds like a fairy tale. I still can't believe it to this day. But don't let the results fool you, this took a lot of trial and error but the coaching was what helped me speed up the learning curb.

It is now my turn to give back. Hopefully this book can be your guiding light to live the life that you have always dreamed of. Now the next sections of the book you do not have to read in order. Each one is divided into the 4 pillars of the Good Life: Health, Wealth, Love, and Happiness and how I began to excel in each. This is when I bring you into my world on an intimate level and tell you things that I don't even tell my close family or friends. In each of the 4 pillars I am going to tell you the story of my journey in each. I want you to follow the Pareto's principle and focus on the one that you need most right now. But just know that focusing on just one will not bring you to a life of fulfillment. So don't forget to review the other pillars as well when the time is right.

I now welcome you into The Lazy Man's Guide to Living The Good Life

Pillar 1: Health

Chapter 9 The bedridden billionaire

You want to make a lot of money? Awesome. But what is the point if you are fat and depressed? Before you embark on a journey to wealth you need to make sure that your health is in check.

"Let us rise up and be thankful, for if we didn't learn a lot today, at least we learned a little, and if we didn't learn a little, at least we didn't get sick, and if we got sick, at least we didn't die; so, let us all be thankful." - Gautama Buddha

Health is our biggest wealth. Don't ever complain that you don't have the money you need when you have the health and the motivation to wake up every day to chase your dreams. Now I want to ask you a question. Who would you rather be, a billionaire that's bedridden and about to die or a broke person that is healthy and alive? No matter how much money you make in your life, you cannot escape death as much as we want to. I would never want to trade my place for that bedridden billionaire because I know no matter what happens in my life or even if I go broke after writing this book, as long as I have my health and the ability to wake up every single morning, I know I can bounce right back up. That should be your mindset as well. You already have all the resources you need to become successful by being alive and healthy, so what is stopping you?

But for others, health is still an issue. No worries because knowing that it is a problem is the first step to fixing the problem. I am going to break down exactly how you can grow your health in body and in mind by sharing with you exactly how I figured out for myself. Now please remember, I am not telling you this as if I were some almighty health being that knows everything, I still splurge a lot every now and then. But where I am now compared to where I was can help inspire you to take on the same journey to getting healthier. That is all these stories are meant to do: not tell you what to do, but inspire you to take action.

Chapter 10 The asthmatic nerd that evolved

I was beaten up by a girl once... In my defense she was a lot bigger than me. I was 8 years old at the time and I just enrolled into Tae Kwon Do because my parents were too worried that I would be picked on. It couldn't be helped. Trust me if you would have seen me as a child you would pick on me too. I was a skinny little boy with bushy hair that resembled an afro, sinus problems galore, and a head that was twice as big as my body. It was one of my first days and for some reason the sensei dude put me up against a girl. Are you serious? Out of all the people here, you put me up against the only girl here? It was a lose lose battle. It is either that I use my ninja skills to disarm this amazon woman of a 10-year-old and lose all credibility I had as a man, or I take the beating and have everyone make fun of me for getting beaten up by a girl. Even though I tried the former, she ended up kicking my ass. Thanks sensei for the much needed confidence boost.

Growing up I was always short and skinny. I had no muscle whatsoever other than my little 4 pack I had going on. But like how big boobs on a fat girl don't count, a six pack on a super skinny dude doesn't count either. My entire life I was picked on due to my skinniness and lack of confidence. I mean can you blame them? I looked like the twig midget version of Bruce Lee.

As I got older, my lack of confidence due to my body started affecting me. I didn't have the ability to stand up for myself, I got made fun of a ton, and I didn't even have the courage to say hi to girls.

It's one thing to want to become successful, but how could I become successful when I wasn't confident in myself?

One day in 8th grade, I got invited to a party of a girl that I liked. I was like hell yes. Oh crap. It was a swimming party. I almost didn't want to go, but I mustered up the courage to end up going anyways. Yay me. I get there and everyone was in their bathing suits. Really? Like I didn't even get a chance to warm up my abs WTF? So while everyone was swimming, I stayed dry right next to the bags of chips. That day I ate two bags of Doritos as an excuse to not going into the pool. As I was going up to talk to the girl that I liked, I saw her talking to my other friend Esteban. He was the size of an NFL linebacker at the ripe age of 13. I was no competition. I know it sounds stupid, but yes I ended up working on my fitness not because of caring for my health like I tell you guys to worry about. I worked on my fitness to build up the confidence to get the girl I liked. More importantly, I wanted confidence in myself.

So began my transformation. Everyday afterwards I began to lift something. It didn't matter what it was, if it was in my reach I would pick it up and put it down. Gallons of milk, furniture, and when my mom brought home groceries, I even attempted to bring all of the bags into the house without taking a second trip. My strength began to grow. Just kidding it didn't but how awesome would that success story be. Boy lifts milk and gets jacked.

Ok on a serious note I ended up hitting the gym. I googled everything that could possibly help me get bigger arms and a bigger upper body. I knew what my motivation was and I hit the gym every single day. Some days I couldn't go so I worked out with my dad's free weights in the basement. One day while doing the bench press with about 60 pounds, the weight ended up getting stuck ontop of me and I couldn't do one more rep to push it up. Now I know this doesn't sound like a lot but when you way less than 120 pounds...

That was like half my body weight! I ended up being stuck there for 20 minutes screaming for help. But my mom was too busy watching her soap operas that no one was able to help their poor little boy out. Eventually my dad heard me and came down to help me out and freed me from my iron prison that was the barbell bar. It was in that moment when I began to change my approach.

As I grew older I ended up giving myself a rule. I would no longer lift alone. Instead I would lift with people who were only stronger than me because I didn't want to end up strangled by the very weight that was supposed to build my confidence. Something weird happened. I ended up putting 40 pounds on of pure muscle (ok there was some fat in there too) within a year.

Looking back, I mean it makes sense. If you go to the gym with someone that is closer to your goals than you are, it pushes you past your comfort zone. That is the fastest way to get the results you want at the gym.

I repeated this process over and over again through the years and have built up a considerable amount of muscle mass and have gotten a whole lot of confidence when compared to who I was back then.

I am now also able to eat whatever I want and still maintain a six-pack! And it is not a skinny boy six pack anymore, it's like a manly-man-dang-I-just-chopped-down-this-tree-with-my-bare-hands   type of six pack.

In the next chapter I will go over the different workouts I did to achieve my goals.

Chapter 11 How I travel the world with a six pack

I did not plan for this. I ended up lifting weights because I wanted more confidence. But now people just hate me. They see the pictures I post on social media and they say things like, "What the fuck Mike, How the hell do you still maintain your physique while traveling and eating like crap?" Well well my friend, it is because I applied the Pareto Principle to my workouts as I know that there are only 20 percent of things I needed to do to maintain my body's health.

The first thing I do is I intermittent fast. In layman's terms intermittent fasting is basically not eating for a period of time. Google it I swear it is healthy. Instead of me going through the scientific mumbo jumbo I am just going to go over the benefits.

1) Helps you lose belly fat
2) Reduces inflammation in the body
3) Promotes cellular repair

And way more that I don't think I am allowed to write about because I am not a doctor and cannot give diet advice. But this is what I ended up doing. All I would do is skip breakfast and then eat my first meal at lunch and go on my day eating normally. I know I know, but your mommy told you that skipping breakfast is bad for you. Don't take my advice for it and just do your dang research if you don't believe me. But after the end of the day doing intermittent fasting I end up still burning more calories from my day to day activities than I was taking in - wala six pack abs without trying.

Terry Crews, an actor from one of my all-time favorite movies White Chicks intermittent fasts... And he is HUGE and cut. So I was like shit. Maybe he is on to something. So I followed the entire process of pushing back my first meal and just drinking a lot of water in the morning. And no matter where I go or how long I travel. I can still enjoy pigging out on the local food while still looking sexy naked... Yolo. Thanks intermittent fasting.

But Mike, maybe it's because of your genetics. Well dude you can use that as an excuses or you can start getting results. But as always consult a doctor before doing anything diet related. Now I want to advise you that I DID NOT STARVE MYSELF. I ate like a normal human being if anything I eat way more. Burgers, Mac and cheese, french fries, you put it in front of me and it would be in my belly in seconds. But that is how science works. Regardless what you eat or what "magical diet" you try next. If you expend more calories than you take in, your body fat percentage would decrease. Just please don't do anything stupid and please do your own research before attempting to intermittent fast from just the information on this page.

But seriously when people ask what it is I do, especially when traveling, it is intermittent fasting.

Another question that people have is how am I also still able to not lose my muscle mass as well? Well of course while traveling, I don't always have a gym available so of course I am going to lose some of it, but there are some aspects of traveling that has actually helped me achieve my fitness goals.

For one, when I am at home I am sitting down and on my laptop. If anyone sits for 8 hours on their laptop of course they will gain weight. It's because they are not expending energy. But when I travel. I walk everywhere, I explore in the mountains, I jump off waterfalls, I am constantly moving. I am expending more energy than someone would at their desk in the office.

Another thing that I do is whenever I have to go to the bathroom (which is frequently throughout the day since I drink a lot of water) I try to do as much push-ups on the floor as possible. Now I know this probably sounds stupid (because it does) but the consistency with staying active and doing that plus going on adventures everyday can have a compounding effect for the better.

For example, if you eat a piece of cake right after reading this book, you will not get fat. However, if you eat a piece of cake everyday right before bed, your actions of you making poor eating decisions will compound and make you fat within 30 days.

How about this, If I were to give you a million dollars or a penny that doubled every single day for 30 days on day 30 which one would you take? Heck yes give me the million most say, but on day 30 the penny ends up to compound to $5,368,709.12. That is more than 5 times what you would have picked if you went with the million. That is the power of compounding and like how the penny had huge effect after the 30 days, the decisions we make with our health everyday can have a drastic effect in 30 days as well. Those couple of push-ups that I do before the bathroom, of course they are not going to get me muscular; but if I were to do it overtime, what do you think would happen just by the effects of compounding? Regardless if you do this or not, every single day you make a decision of either compounding your health for the better or for the worse. Even if you don't make a decision, that is still a decision in itself that would compound for the worse.

So this is my secret to maintaining my physical health. Now I want to ask you…

Who are people that have the fitness results you want?

Ask them if they would go to the gym with you

What is one habit you can create for yourself that you would do every day that could compound into something greater for your health? (it doesn't have to be doing push-ups whenever you go potty, I am just weird)

Now when I am not traveling (or if I stay in one place for more than a month), one way I use to rapidly increase my progress is I hit the gym 3 times a week. I don't run around without a plan spending hours and hours at the gym just to get small results. No. I am way more efficient. For one, I only stay at the gym for less than 45 minutes. Anything longer and you just end up getting lazy and talking to friends or sitting their texting on your phone.

I focus only on compound movements in the rep range of 5 reps for 5 sets. This is what helps me build up the testosterone I need while cutting down my time at the gym so I can focus on more important things other than being a gym rat.

The next thing I focus on is called the "Tabata Protocol". You can google it for all the awesome mumbo jumbo. But the awesome thing about it is that it can burn calories up to 12 hours after the workout. And that is not even the best part... The best part is that it is 4 minutes long. Yep 4 minutes. But those 4 minutes are hell. Make sure you warm up before you do this. What I do is go on one of those bikes they have at the gym and download a tabata protocol app timer that is available for free on any smart phone. You press start and for 20 seconds you go all out as fast as you can, and when you think you cannot go any faster.. Push yourself a little more. Then after the 20 seconds is up the timer will beep and you have 10 seconds of rest. Once the timer beeps again you go as fast as you can for the 20 seconds again and you repeat the process until the 8 minutes are up.

Don't worry if you look like an idiot. That's how you're supposed to look when doing the tabata protocol. Oh and if you are able to walk properly after one of these exercises... You did it wrong. How this works is the rapid amount of energy you use in a short amount of time puts your body at an oxygen deficit. This is because all of your blood sugar has been burned off in the rapid burst of exercise you do in a short amount of time. With all your blood sugar depleted and your cells still need energy, your body takes it from burning your fat even long after the workout is done. Doing this just 3 times a week can turn your body into a fat burning machine and is one of the reasons why I am able to run around eating like a pig with a six pack.

I remember back in the day, I would literally spend hours and hours at the gym. Always trying to be the biggest dude there and just wanting the validation from my fellow peers on my size. But guess what? I was not living. Just like how staying at a job for 8 hours a day is not living... Staying in the gym for anything longer than an hour is just a waste of your precious life. So during the time where I do go to the gym this is the sample workout I do to get me into the best shape as possible with the least amount of effort.

Day 1: Chest
Incline Bench: 5 sets of 5 reps
Dumbbell Press: 5 sets of 5 reps
Overhead Press: 5 sets of 5 reps
Lateral Raises: 5 sets of 12 reps
Tabata Protocol exercise: 4 minutes

Day 2: Back
Weighted Pull Ups: 5 sets of 5 reps
Bent over Rows: 5 sets of 5 reps
Weighted Pull downs: 5 sets of 5 reps

Bent Over Lateral Raises: 5 sets of 12 reps
Tabata Protocol exercise: 4 minutes

Day 3: Legs
Squats: 5 sets of 5 reps
Deadlifts: 5 sets of 5 reps
Calves: 5 sets of 20 reps
Tabata Protocol exercise: 4 minutes

Mix the above workout with intermittent fasting and you can spend less time in the gym and more time living your life on your own terms. Also don't forget to give yourself a lot of rest because this workout will for sure kick your ass and make you feel sore.

Chapter 12 Your first hour

So as I was building my business, the hardest part in the beginning was keeping my attention on it. If you have ever built something of your own, you know what I am talking about. You would have a to-do list of all the things you need to do today, but things at work may get in the way, distractions may come up, and before you know it that long list of to do things are carried over to the next day where nothing still gets done.

Getting your body healthy is one thing... Getting your mind healthy is another...

This was so hard for me to get over and it seemed it was because my mind was always filled with clutter. If that is the case, how can I build my business and more importantly my future when I have all this nonsense in my brain clouding my judgment?

Now what I am about to tell you may sound kind of weird. Especially if you are new to this success thing. But the biggest thing that changed my life (I kid you not) is devoting the first hour of my day to myself.

"Mike, what the hell do you mean devote the first hour of my day to myself?"

If you think about it, every day you wake up and you are constantly reacting to the environment. You check emails, you check text messages, you check social media, and you respond to all these people and putting their needs over your own.

I know this because I was a victim of this. Every morning I would wake up and I would check my emails. It would be filled with things that other people wanted me to do for the day. And within 5 minutes of waking up I was already feeling stressed.

Can you imagine how the feeling of being stressed affected my decision making for that day? Would it fuel me or would it hurt me from making the choices I need to make?
Being in a stressful state is the worst, especially if you are building a business on the side of working a job, caring for a family, or just caught up with the busyness of life. So what I do for the first one hour of waking up... Is devoting that hour all to myself. My biggest goal for the first hour of every day is to put my body in the most positive state of being that I could. The reason for this is because you cannot build a positive life with a negative mindset. You need to force yourself in a positive state because it is in this state of being when you can make the best decisions for your life. It will also allow you to act on faith instead of reacting to fear.

So this is how I do it. I'm telling you this right now it will sound weird and almost crazy. But hey if you are struggling with starting your day off right then I would recommend this.

The moment I wake up; I leap out of bed. Why? Most people press the snooze button over and over again. These are the people that don't want to face with the challenges of the day. If you do this, you are convincing your mind that doing the work that you need to do today is something you do not want to do. And if you keep on going with this mindset, you will quickly begin to hate the business you are in. Immediately after, without looking at my phone of course (as it is shut off for the first hour of the day), I drink a huge glass of water. Most people feel groggy and depressed in the morning, but you know what is crazy? It's because you're dehydrated. The human brain is 85% water and you were just asleep for 8 hours. If you wonder why you aren't as alert in the morning, it's because you don't have the water you need to take on the day. Most people just choke down coffee and get on with their day always wondering why the coffee always ends up losing its effect so quickly. If you do this one thing alone, and just commit to drink a shit ton of water in the morning, you will do so much for your energy levels that you will be able to take anything on.

The next thing I do is I sit down and quiet my mind. Did you know that we have about 70,000 thoughts a day? That is 70,000 opportunities to discourage you from taking action. You need to tell your mind who is the boss and control what it is you think. Every great book on success always talks about how "your thoughts become things" and it is true. What you think about is what will come about, but it is so hard when you discourage yourself 70,000 times throughout the day. So how I quiet my mind is after immediately drinking water, I sit down in a quiet place and just think of 3 things that I am grateful for. It doesn't have to be anything big, it can be as small as being grateful for your heart, for your ability to see, for the ability to wake up. There is a power in waking up and filling your day with gratitude before your day has begun.

"Better to lose count while naming your blessings than to lose your blessings to counting your troubles" - Maltbie D. Babcock

Stop focusing on the things you don't have, and start appreciating the things you already have. We take for granted many things and we tend to not appreciate them until they are gone. Something as small as being thankful for your eyesight when many people are waking up to complete darkness gives you this feeling of abundance that is hard to explain in words.

The next thing that you want to do is focus on 3 people that you are grateful for. I think about their faces and them smiling as weird as it sounds. I also wish that they have a good day in my mind. So many people get caught up with work and business that they lose touch with their family because they forgot just how much they mean to them when they are lost in the daily hustle. Ever met a businessman who didn't end up knowing their kids? How about a loving mom that focuses so hard on giving the life they want their child to have, but end up being overwhelmed with working overtime that the child grows up not knowing her mom?

The next thing I want you to do is to visualize 3 goals that you want to obtain. But visualize them as if you already have them. Your thoughts, your actions, and your results are all connected. If you start thinking like the person you are when you are worth a million bucks, you will start adapting your habits to how someone with a million bucks would act. It is getting yourself in the right mindset to take the right action that will get you the results. So tricking your mind every single day will start to get your daily actions closer to that of your ideal self... Your best version of yourself that deserves the best possible life.

How would it feel if you had already accomplished your goal?
What would your ideal life look like?
How are your loved ones reacting to your success?
What emotions do they feel knowing that you accomplished your goal?
How proud and confident do you now feel in yourself?

Now I know this all sounds weird to many of you but I am telling you it is this very state I put myself every single morning.

Even doing this for just 10 minutes within waking up can change your life completely for the better. It will give you the focus you need to take the action that you have to take that day. It will give you the clarity that is necessary to take on your goals.

Try it for just 21 days and let me know if it has changed your life, your mood, and your relationships in that short amount of time. And for all the people complaining saying that they do not have the time...

As my friend Tony Robbins would say - "If you don't have 10 minutes for yourself, you don't have a life"

Pillar 2: WEALTH

Chapter 13 (Do you really want to build a business...)

"Everyone wants to go to heaven but nobody wants to die" - Joe Louis

So you want to become wealthy huh? Well you are going to have to make some sacrifices and do some work. Just like how Joe Louis says, "Everyone wants to go to heaven but nobody wants to die," everyone wants to live the good life, but so few are willing to work for it. Why? Because it's hard man. Growing a business in the beginning without any background knowledge is hard work. If it was easy everyone would do it. But the fact that it is not easy should excite the hell out of you because the level of difficulty kills off your competition that doesn't have the courage and the faith to know that the life of entrepreneurship is way better than the life of indentured servitude and spiritual suicide.

No business is easy... If somebody tells you how easy a business is, do yourself a favor and run the other way. Building a business takes a lot of time, money, and effort to figure out how to make it grow.

Do you have what it takes to actually build a business? You probably don't as of right now, but don't worry. I am going to break down some concepts that are going to give your brain some entrepreneurial steroids later on in this section of the book.

Before you start on your journey, you need to know the reason you want to become successful. And no I don't mean the "I want to make more money" or "I want to help people" bullshit. What is the REAL reason why you want to become successful? What would pull you out of bed every single morning? What would motivate you through all the hard times and challenges? What is the reason why you are currently breathing?

You see most people are so strung up on the "How." They ask themselves questions like "how am I going to do this" or "how am I going to do that" and they focus so much on the vehicle that when a hard battle comes their way, they end up quitting before their journey even began. But you want to know a secret? If the why is big enough, the how doesn't matter.

For example, if someone came up to you and asked for $10,000 in the next 24 hours, would you be able to find the resources to come up with that kind of money in time? No? Most people don't have $1000 laying around much less $10,000. Ok what if this random person had your loved ones captive with a gun to each one of their heads... And they said if you don't show up with $10,000 in the next 24 hours all your loved ones would end up dying right before your eyes. Would you be able to find the $10,000 now? Or would you just give up and say sorry mom and dad couldn't find the money... See you on the other side.

Now I know this is a pretty extreme example, but it shows what I am trying to say perfectly. Our biggest problem in creating wealth isn't that we don't have the resources for wealth. It's that we lack the resourcefulness to get the resources, and that is because we lack motivation.

A mentor once told me this example and it opened up my eyes on what I was willing to do to come up with the money to save my family. It didn't matter how. I was going to come up with the money one way or another to save my loved ones.

When you find something that motivates you to take action every single day, you no longer feel forced or pressured to take the day's challenges head on. Instead, you feel as if you are unstoppable and no matter what gets in your way, it doesn't matter because your "why" is greater than your "pain." Take this time right now to write your "why." It sounds dumb, I know. I thought the same thing. But when someone that was more successful than me told me to do it, I stopped asking questions and I started to write down my damn why. So you should too.

When you pick the vehicle to wealth later on in this book, there are many times that you are just going to want to give up, crawl in a ball, and cry. Seeing your why written on a piece of paper will remind you that you're not in this business to make yourself feel good. You are in this business to make a fucking difference for you and the people you care about. Suddenly your bullshit story that you tell yourself on why you can't accomplish all that you deserve will be overwhelmed with the motivation and the desire to make shit happen because your why is so big. So when I tell you to take 10 minutes to write down your fucking why... DO IT.

Put it right by your bedside and read it every single morning and every single night. Why am I telling you to do this? BECAUSE I FUCKING DID IT. Yes, that is right, your boy Mike Vestil back in the day in college would have a piece of paper attached by his bedside, whose roommates thought he was crazy for reading the same piece of paper over and over again every single day, I wrote down my why and it was my why that led me to this life.

Every time I read that piece of paper it was if a fire was lit under my ass. I wrote how I did not want my mom to work 16 hour days anymore, I wrote that I did not want my sister to go through the same emotional and financial turmoil as I did going through college, and I did not want my dad to have to work the night shift so he can actually spend time with my mom. Now every time I wanted to give up, I read that piece of paper and I grinded out passed the point where most people usually quit.

Now it is your turn.

What is your why?

Take ten minutes to write it down before going on to the next chapter. And remember if you don't, the only person you are cheating is yourself. Don't rob yourself the motivation you need to succeed. Write that shit down.

Chapter 14 Train your mind

I remember so many instances when I would first begin on my journey that I felt like giving up. I would feel disbelief in myself, I would lose confidence, and I would always ask myself if working this hard for no results was worth the struggle. It was so hard for me to believe that this was possible for me because I had no prior results whatsoever.

Success never comes easy and I had to be willing to do things that most sane people wouldn't. I would sleep later than everyone else, and I would wake up much earlier. When all my friends would go out and get drunk on the weekends, I stayed in and read books. When everyone was living their life with the final years of college I was being a loner and growing my mind. The entrepreneur life in the beginning is sad but don't worry it gets better.

You have to do what others won't so you can live how others can't. Many people back in the day would tell me, "Mike, enjoy yourself stop working so hard... College is the best 4 years of your life so enjoy it while it lasts." In my mind I was thinking, "Hell no... how can college be the best 4 years of my life when I still have 60 more years left to live?" I refused to only have fun for that amount of time.

So every day I would commit to growing my mind. Why? Because the universe doesn't just give anybody a million dollars. For you to earn a million dollars, you need to become the person that deserves a million dollars.

Ever notice when someone wins the lottery... That within a couple years they are either broke, depressed, or dead? That is because they didn't deserve the success so of course they are going to lose it.

"If someone gives you $1,000,000 you'd better become a millionaire so you can keep the money. Success doesn't want to hang around incompetent people." - Jim Rohn

In other words, you don't get out of life what you want. You get out of life who you are by the person that you become. In the same way that lottery winners end up losing all their money in a short amount of time, what happens to millionaires that lose their money?

Donald Trump has been bankrupt multiple times... But since he knew his worth, he was always able to recoup his billionaire status because that is who he is.

You see success is kind of like a thermostat with a set temperature. Whenever it gets too cold, the heater turns on and it brings it back to normal level. And whenever it gets too hot, the air conditioning turns on and brings it back down to normal level. This is just like success. Many people have their own set point for success. For someone that just wins the lottery and hasn't gone through the challenges and the failures one would take on getting success, they end up losing it all because their set point is low on the success thermostat. When a millionaire or a billionaire loses everything, they still manage to gain their success back if not even more because they learned a lesson from their failures; A millionaire's success thermostat is set much higher.

Your goal, especially when starting off is to start increasing your set point higher than you are comfortable with. The best way to do that is to brainwash yourself. That is right brainwashing. I don't know if you know this but we have been brainwashed ever since we were young. Let's see if you can fill out the blanks with your mind.

Go to school to get good _____
Graduate, and get a _____
Work really really hard until you _____

How most people read it "Go to school to get a good GRADES, graduate, and get a JOB, work really really hard until you RETIRE"

You know what is messed up? Most people in the last blank thought it was "Work really really hard until you DIE"

Which is eerily true in most cases...

If you were able to fill in just one of the blanks... you have sadly been brainwashed by society. This happened to me so I needed to rewire my brain. I knew the only way for me to earn more was to BECOME more. I had to immerse myself around successful people. Even though I did not have any time at all to grow my mind I committed to doing this minimum every single day

Habit #1: Read 10 pages of a book on success
Habit #2: Listen to 30 minutes of an audio book on success

This was my way of brainwashing myself. And if you really think about it, it makes sense. Any success book will tell you that thoughts become things. Well if someone that was far more successful than me decided to write down their entire life lessons and failures in a book then that is like cheating life if I were too read it. You can get 80 years of knowledge in a span of 100 pages. Not only do you get to learn from these author's failures, you get to start adapting the thoughts that they would think. Now if they have the results you want and thoughts really do become things, then by the transitive property, wouldn't you say that if you thought the same thoughts as successful people, then you would end up gaining the same things?

"The reading of all good books is like a conversation with the finest minds of past centuries" - Descartes

How hard would it be to just read 10 pages of a good book of someone that has the results you want a day?
What about listening to 30 minutes of audio of someone that had the results you wanted?

If you think about it people spend hours of their time commuting to and from work. What if you use that time to start growing your mind?

Just try this for 21 days and even if you end up quitting whatever business you may start. You will have been bitten by the entrepreneurial bug... And there will be no turning back.

If you want to get an update to the current books I am reading and the audiobooks I am listening to just head on over to **www.mikevestil.com/books**

Chapter 15 Finding your vehicle

One of my biggest problems when beginning my journey was finding the vehicle that was going to bring me the wealth I wanted. I thought that I had to invent the next Uber or create the next Facebook and I was always stressed wondering why I wasn't smart enough to think of something that could make me money. The reason why I could never figure it out was because I was looking in the wrong places. I was trying to CREATE something new instead of following what ALREADY WORKS.

A mentor wants told me, "Mike, if you want something in life you have to find someone that has what you want, say what they say, do what they do, get what they have every single time." I mean it makes sense doesn't it? When you want to be good at basketball would you listen to Michael Jordan or your friend who has never dribbled a ball before? If a fat person was trying to give you tips on how to lose weight, would you even consider his advice? I don't think so. Even though this is the case, many of us has fallen victim to people's advice that DO NOT have the results we want. Yet we listen to them over and over again especially when it comes to being "successful" in life. What blows my mind is I one time took a business class where the professor was giving me tips on how to make a million dollars. But how the hell can he give me advice if he was only making $60K a year? Sorry professor I am going to have to politely say screw off to your advice.

How I found my vehicle is I found someone who had the success that I wanted and paid him to teach me.

"But Mike, aren't you afraid he might scam you?" And to that I would say it would be a scam if he didn't charge me. It would be a scam to my time being wasted learning things that are not proven to work if he did not charge me. If you think about it you pay an institution $30K-60K a year for 4 years to maybe one day come out with a $30K a year salary. The scary thing is that this salary IS NOT GUARANTEED since people are having a harder time finding a job right after college. What's fucked up is there is no "return policy" once you spent that money there is no going back. And you can't even declare bankruptcy like you would if you bought a house. No... you're what I like to call royally fucked. If this is you, instead of whining about it, find a mentor like I did and kiss his feet for him/her to teach you.

So yes... I ended up paying this mentor $1400 for him to coach me (nothing when you compare it to the cost of college) and he taught me his exact vehicle which was as you know selling weird t-shirts online. Unlike someone who didn't have the results I wanted, Charlie was able to tell me exactly where I was messing up in my business because he went through the same failures. So he easily knew what was wrong and showed me how to fix it.

Here is the cliff notes of exactly what he taught me.

He told me, "Mike, in any business you need to focus on three important things: 1) The People 2) The Product 3) The Promotion"

The people is the passionate audience that you are trying to sell stuff too. Also known as a niche. There are certain niches that are hungrier than others and your goal is to give them what they already want. If you want the niches that he recommended when I started off you can get them at **www.mikevestil.com/20niches**.

The product is the actual thing you are selling. It needs to resonate with the niche that you are selling to. In whatever business you are in, if you put the wrong product in front of the right niche or the right product in front of the wrong niche, you will not get any sales. No sales. No money. Mastering how to connect the passionate niches with the products that they ALREADY WANT was one of the biggest skills Charlie taught me.

The promotion is how you get the product in front of people that already want it. You can have the best product in the world, but if no one sees it no one will buy it. There are many ways to do this ranging from Google Ads, Social Media Marketing, Facebook Ads, Word of Mouth, Email Marketing... There is an infinite amount of traffic sources out there that goes far beyond the scope of this book that you can use to promote the products to the right people. If you download the 20 niches in the link above, I go over some of these traffic sources in more depth with live trainings so make sure you download the niches when you have the time.

These are the only 3 concepts you need to build your business from the ground up. So I would recommend focusing in on these whenever starting any business. That is what I did. I picked a couple of niches that I understood, I did my research, and I found out exactly what it is the particular audience wanted in a product. The next step was finding out where all the people that liked this particular product was hanging out. I found out that there were a lot of Facebook pages, Facebook groups, and Instagram pages that were devoted to these niches so I knew that it was a popular niche. I also was able to find out where the people were hanging out so I know where it is to sell them the product. What do I mean by this? Well say if your audience is vegetarians and you are at a vegetarian convention, it would make no sense to sell T shirts saying "I Love Hamburgers" when everyone at the convention are vegetarians. Well with the audience that you want to sell to, they collect in certain places on the internet. Your goal is to find out where these places are and that is where you do your promotion. Don't waste your time doing a promotion in a place that doesn't have your audience congregating. Then you would be just like the person selling I love hamburger shirts at a vegetarian convention. The next thing you want to do is use whatever promotion you can do to get your product in front of those people. You can use advertising and pay someone like Facebook to put your product in front of the people, or you can find someone on Instagram that already has your ideal audience following them and pay them to showcase your shirt to their people. Either way, promotion is where the money is made. When the product and the people are congruent with each other, promoting it in the right way is the fastest way to sales.

I repeated this process for multiple niches and that was the base of my success. You can try this route if you would like to but remember this is NOT THE ONLY ROUTE. There are hundreds of opportunities out there you just have to keep an open mind. Don't be one of those people that calls something a scam when you don't understand it. Do your research, follow people that have the results that you want, and follow where people are making money and don't worry if there is competition. Competition just means there is money being made and competition shows that there is opportunity. If you want other options to creating success, I have an email newsletter where I get guest speakers who are the most successful in their niche to come and do live trainings to teach you exactly what it is they know so you can cut your learning curb. For everyone that downloads the 20 niches at www.mikevestil.com/20niches I send about one live training a month to help you guys figure out what vehicle is best for you if selling t shirts isn't for you, so make sure you get that download.

Chapter 16 Building a team

I was sitting in front of the TV watching Netflix for 16 hours a day, I kid you not. I would just watch episode after episode while doing my product research. I would spend all my time creating new advertising campaigns and I was getting more and more depressed. I began to realize what was the point of leaving my career when I just fell into another one? What is the point of leaving an 8-hour job just to get stuck in a 16-hour job? I knew I needed to do something different.

One thing that one of my mentors told me was find out what parts of your business that you do not like doing and hire somebody else to do it for you. So that is exactly what I did I looked at my entire business as a whole and found out I didn't like to do any of it. Which is hard because that is what made me my income. But my long term goal was to remove myself from the equation. To completely separate myself from my earning potential.

I wanted to travel the world, I wanted to live a life where I can just hang out with my family instead of stressing about customer service, I wanted to enjoy freedom. But the way my business was set up, I was the bottleneck that was preventing it from growing. So this is exactly what I did.

I divided the entire business out into categories. The categories were: product research, creating advertising campaigns, managing advertising campaigns, uploading new products, creating new products, and customer service. I looked at the entire thing and was like shit. I am literally working 6 jobs at once. I found the one that annoyed me the most (which was customer service) and I created a DMO aka daily method of operation.

For the next week I recorded on a piece of paper exactly what I did for customer service. I wrote down step by step from how many times I checked the email, how did I respond to the email, and how did I handle the requests they asked me from the email. After compiling the list, I did two things. Number 1, I found out that many of the emails were all asking the same damn thing, so I created a giant frequently asked question list that I could just copy and paste as a response. Number 2, I used this software called Camtasia and recorded my computer screen on how I responded to the email requests on each of the issues they were having and I started to have a data bank of video tutorials. So now I had 3 things ready and done for customer service: 1) the DMO for customer service 2) the FAQ and 3) the video tutorials.

The next thing I needed to do was to hire someone to work for me. But guess what? As a new business I HAD NO MONEY. I didn't want to pay someone $9/hour to do this work.. I would end up broke. So what I ended up doing is utilizing what Tim Ferris author of the 4 Hour Work Week calls geoarbitrage. What it means in this sense is you take the money in a first world country and spend it in a third world country where your dollar will have far more value to the local people.

For example, in the Philippines, the average monthly salary is $200-300 a month. This is the amount of money that can support an entire family over there. So what I did is the moment I started getting a little bit of profit, I ended up finding someone to do customer service for around that much a month and almost instantly I won back several hours of my time per day. I gave them the DMO the FAQ and the video tutorials and they had everything they needed to do customer service.

Ok awesome, now that I had that done, my next goal was to focus on growing revenue and getting more profit. I knew that the more I can profit, the more I can hire out people to do the job for me, so that is exactly what I did. Every time I had more profit in the bank, instead of blowing it off on bottle service or fancy cars and watches. I reinvested it into the business. When you start getting your success, don't do something stupid like buying something you don't need to impress people you don't like. Remember you are in this for the long run. Take that damn money and hire people out so you don't have to sit there like a slave. So one by one I repeated the process for what I did with customer service with each and every job. And after a couple months of doing this for each job that I wanted to outsource to someone else in the Philippines, I ended up getting my time back. What was weird is I had more time and more money doing less than I did when I was doing more. That is because the people that I hired were smart as hell!

The takeaway you should get from this is the moment you start getting any success: instead of getting lost and creating yourself another job, ask yourself how you can make yourself obsolete as fast as possible. I am telling you this right now, my team that works with me is amazing. They are talented and intelligent individuals whose skills are far greater than my own. I am truly grateful for every single one of them.

Once I year I go visit all 8 of them. It is amazing that because of my existence and the business I built I have given 8 families the ability to spend more time with each other since they all work from their laptops. It humbles me to see just how much they appreciate the opportunity, and it also drives me to take massive action so that I can always provide them with a job. I am telling you this right now, the moment you are responsible for somebody else's paycheck and their ability to support their family, something inside of you gets kicked into overdrive and makes you want to create the biggest most stable company possible, not just for your freedom but for theirs as well.

At one point I was doing all 8 of their jobs and I was depressed and unhappy. But now I have divided the work amongst them and all are able to work in their free time since they are all salaried. They are all happy to grow together in this company with me.

The most important thing though is I was able to finally get my time back. Now I have a question for you.

Which one would you rather be?

Someone who living in New York who makes $100,000 a year working 60 hours a week? Or someone living in the Philippines only making $30,000 a year but only works 4 hours a week?

The reason why you want to build a team regardless if you end up taking a pay cut is because it gives you more free time. Couple that with vacationing in a cheaper country that $30,000 a year in the Philippines would make you feel like a millionaire. In fact you would be a millionaire because $1 equals 50 Filipino pesos. You would be raking in 1,500,000 pesos a year. Imagine the life that you would live.

If you are on your way and already building your business... What jobs in your business do you despise? There is someone who would kill to work for you and do the job that you hate. Giving you the free time you need to focus on the bigger aspects of your business like the vision on seeing where you want it to go.

Chapter 17 What do I do with my profits?

Spend it on coke, strippers, and whores of course. Just kidding. Seriously take a joke. This is exactly what I do with it regardless how much profit I make. The first thing I do is to take account how much I am already spending. How much is my cost of rent, how much do I spend per month traveling, how much do I spend eating out. I record everything. Once I have that number (and of course taking taxes into consideration) I ended up creating an LLC, limited liability company in the USA, and I pay myself that specific salary.

"But Mike, I am profiting so much? Why can't I buy the house I always wanted or the car I dreamed of?" Because kid... You will end up going broke in no time.

Did you know within 2 years, about 80% of former NFL players go bankrupt?! These people have made MILLIONS in their career, yet how come shortly after they are done playing sports, they end up losing everything they have ever created. This is because of lifestyle inflation. This gets the best of us. The moment your income tends to go up, your spending habits will tend to go up as well. This keeps on happening as your income grows and soon enough it becomes a habit. What is happening to these NFL players is that they are so used to spending so much money because they thought they had an infinite amount of wealth; but the moment income from their career stopped coming in, they lost it all because they did not know how to live a life without spending the amount of money they are used to.

I am telling you this right now. If you are on this journey to wealth, one of the first things you need to learn it to focus on long term gains instead of short term gains. Pay yourself a fucking salary like I did so you are not tempted to doing something stupid. Pay yourself exactly what it is you need to support you so you do not end up going broke if some unforeseen event forces you to lose your business.

The second thing you want to do with your profits you should be already familiar with and that is reinvesting it into your business, hiring employees, spending it on product research and development, innovating, etc. This should be a given especially if you want to scale your business to huge heights.

Now I want you to pay attention on what I want you to do with the rest of your profit after you are done paying yourself a salary and reinvesting the profits. Around 10% of the profits that you make in your business should go into investing into your brain. It is the best return you can possibly get for your money.

As my business grows, I repeatedly ask myself how I can take 10% of the profits and use it to invest in mentors, in live seminars, and in traveling to do one on one coaching. Your business and its revenue is a direct representation of how much you grow as a person. If your business has become stagnant that is because YOU have become stagnant and stopped focusing on your own internal growth.

Even to this day, as I'm writing this, I have already invested tens of thousands of dollars into growing my brain, learning from mentors, and just constantly pushing myself to improve. I can't tell you how many times I was hesitant to spend that money on finding mentors who charge upwards of $5,000 for them to teach me what they know, but I am telling you this right now, the reason for my success at an early age and the reason why my students wonder why I am wise beyond my years is because I take a good portion of my profits and I use it to grow my mind.

If you noticed in this book I have mentioned several mentors, and that is because I practice what I preach. The more mentors you can have in particular areas in your life that you want improvement be it sales, marketing, personal development, leadership. Spend that money that you have been making and invest it in growing your skills. That is the fastest way for you to blow up any business you have into the next level.

A mentor once told me, "Mike you spend, $20 on a haircut to look good but you can't spend $10 on a book?" Stop spending money outside your head and start spending it on what's on the inside.

The hardest part with investing the profits into yourself and your own personal growth is keeping up with actually spending it all the more you make. Right now I find it difficult to spend my profits on personal growth but yet I still am able to. I devour books and audiobooks on the daily, I attend live seminars every couple months, and I have spent a fortune on one on one coaching from people that are better than me in areas I want improvement in. But remember you do not have to spend tens of thousands like I have. You can simply start by investing the small amount of profits you may be getting in a good book or an audiobook. It's as simple as that.

Now comes the fun part. With the rest of your profit. You should put it all into index funds.

"By periodically investing in an index fund, the know-nothing investors can actually outperform most investment professionals." - Warren Buffet

So what is an index fund?

"An index fund is a type of mutual fund with a portfolio constructed to match or track the components of a market index, such as the

Standard & Poor's 500 Index (S&P 500). An index mutual fund is said to provide broad market exposure, low operating expenses and low portfolio turnover."

But if the above statement doesn't make any sense to you. Just understand that they can grow anywhere from 5% to 10% a year. Meaning if you have $100,000 in it… You can make anywhere from $5,000 to $10,000 a year EXTRA without doing shit. Seriously. So your biggest goal is to make as much in a business and put a good chunk of it into an index fund that can fund the lifestyle that you want..

Chapter 18 What is your dream life?

I want you to take a second and write down the dream life you want. What is the car you are driving? What is the house you are living in? What are the vacations you are taking? Write down everything you have ever wanted. Now that you have a list of things that you want, write down the price it would take to have each. Most people believe that they need a billion dollars to be happy. But you can live your dream life for as little as $8,000 a month

For example, here is one of my students dream lives:

Living in an apartment in Manhattan: $1700 to $3500/month

Leasing a Lambo: $2700 (I know I know you are supposed to buy a lambo not lease it but just pay attention for the example)

Dining out every day: $1500

One monthly vacation to anywhere in the world for a week: $2000

This is around $8,000 a month cost. Now that you know how much your dream life cost let's go back to the index funds that we talked about in the last chapter.

For this particular student he would be able to live the life he wants for $8,000 a month that is around $96,000 a year. Remember how I told you that an index fund can grow from about 5%-10% a year? Well if you put $1 million in an index fund, if your growth for that year is 10% you would have earned $100,000 for that year without even working... Thus funding your dream life. Where the poor work for their money, the rich make their money work for them. If NFL players simply knew how to invest their excess wealth in a safe index fund that grows passively even in your sleep then they would never have to worry about money their entire life, even after retiring from Football.

Guess what though? With the power of the internet and online businesses $1 million is getting more realistic for more and more people every day. The hardest part is just getting the initial amount of success so that you can live passively from the growth of your index fund for the rest of your life. And remember if you need help generating that first part of your wealth you can get some of my ideas at www.mikevestil.com/20niches .

Some of the action steps you can do now is define the cost of your dream life. Once you know exactly how much it costs find out how much you need in an index fund so you can safely live off of its growth. Once you have that idea, create an online business and make it a goal to save up that amount so that you can begin to live the lifestyle you want. Creating an online business and living off of index funds is one of the most important aspects in the Lazy Man's guide to living the good life. Because the moment the amount of money you saved hits critical mass, it will continue to grow and grow for ever and ever. Giving you more time to focus on the more important things in your life.

Pillar 3: LOVE

Chapter 19 What is love?
Baby don't hurt me

Ok so I really didn't want to write this chapter because there were so many times in my life that I suffered from feeling loneliness. And I get it it sucks. But hopefully my experience in growing in this pillar can really help you go through what ever difficulties you are going through with your relationships.

No amount of health and wealth in the world is worth it if you end up dying alone without the feeling of truly being loved unconditionally. It really is a weird human need that can take over our senses and render our logic useless. From the feeling of butterflies in your stomach when meeting someone that you could potentially fall in love, to the feeling of regret and remorse seeing yourselves falling out of love... The entire experience is an emotional roller coaster that doesn't entirely make sense. But it is not supposed to. Just know that with all the ups and downs it's all a part of life. Even just knowing about it can save you so much heart ache and pain down the road.

It's been said that everyone will experience 3 loves in their life. The love that was your first heartbreak, the love that was perfect but was at the wrong time, and the love that you don't see coming but is the one that will last a lifetime. This is my journey.

Chapter 20 Enter Love #1

It was high school year and I was running around being the weirdo that I was. It was around the time that I was experimenting with my self-identity so at this particular moment in my life I had a buzz cut, eyebrow piercing, and green contact lenses.

I had recently started working out so my confidence was slowly getting better. On top of that I wore smaller t shirts because I thought that it would make me look more muscular. But rather it just made me look like I was trying so hard - which I was.

A lot of people didn't know what to do with me since I drastically changed my appearance and personality because I didn't really know who I was. This confused everyone else around me and pushed me further away from being one of the "cool kids." I was an outcast, with only a few really close friends and a bunch of just mere "acquaintances." It was cool though, I was a happy kid and I guess that is all that really matters.

I had no idea what she saw in me, but after meeting her I was thrown head over heels. It was a cold Friday night in the fall semester of Junior Year of high school, and everyone that attended the school would show up to go to these football games. We were known to be really good one year, and really sucky the next year. This particular year we were doing horrible. It didn't matter though; everyone was meeting up at the football game as a place to hang out - most people actually didn't watch the football game.

And that was when I saw her. She was a 5 foot 6 girl with long dirty blonde hair that was closer to brunette. She was wearing tight yoga pants and a hoodie with the name of our high school right across her chest. The moment I saw her, she immediately noticed and gave me the strongest eye contact I have ever received. At that moment I felt excited yet uncomfortable. I wanted to look away but I couldn't stop staring. Before I knew it we were both smiling and in my mind I was thinking who the hell is this girl.

I of course didn't have the courage to go and say hi so I did everything else to get her attention. I would go by my friends that were around her vicinity and pretend to laugh really loud and fake having a good time so she would wonder what was going on - don't worry it didn't work. I tried making her jealous by talking to my female friends and trying to get her to see me hugging them so that she would know just how much of a prime piece of meat I was when she saw all these girls (ok it was one girl and she was slightly chubby) hugging me - didn't work. So I was freaking out wondering if this was the last time I was going to see her, so I did what any boy in the middle of puberty would do.

I went over to the food stand, bought some hot cocoa, pretended to walk buy her, and then pretended to fall with the hot cocoa causing a huge massive scene (I told you I was really trying to figure out my identity). I then poked fun at her blaming her for tripping me and spilling my hot chocolate and she just ended up laughing and calling me out for the dumb shit I just attempted to pull. Either way, even though she thought I was weird, she did think I was cute so we went over to the food stand and we split a cup of hot cocoa. She told me her name was Rebecca and she was a Sophomore.

I ended up taking her on a double date with my friend the next week because I had no courage to do it by myself and it was one of the most awkward first dates ever. For one, I had no idea what the hell to say. In my opinion, taking a girl to the movies is the worst thing you can do. It's quiet, you can't talk, and the entire time you are awkwardly trying to put your arm around her which to them just feels

94

straight up weird. I could tell she was losing interest. I had to pull a Hail Mary. After the movie, me and my friend converse in the bathroom and I say "dude, I don't think she likes me" and my friend politely responded "Shut the fuck up man and man up.. You got this" and that is when I had my idea. I decided to take the date to Taco Bell where I would wow Rebecca with my somewhat decent Spanish skills. Either way, I think it was me being weird that got her so attracted to me. Which works out well for me because I am as weird as it gets.

She shortly became my girlfriend right after. And not just any girlfriend, my first ever Facebook official girlfriend. Right from the beginning I wanted to be the best boyfriend possible so I went overboard with EVERYTHING to make her fall more and more in love with me every day. I remember every single day we would talk on the phone and waited for each other to go to bed, and she even made me sandwiches in the morning which helped with my muscle gains. I didn't know what the hell love was at that time (heck I don't even know if I know what it is now) but I felt like I was falling more and more in love every single day.

You probably already realize this by now... But I am like that awkward dude that you see in the romantic comedy movies that tries to overdo little cute things and blow them out of proportion. I remember a couple weeks before asking Rebecca out to the Homecoming dance she was freaking out because all her friends have already been asked and she still wasn't. I wanted to make things very interesting.

I got really close with her mom a couple weeks back and she distracted Rebecca and took her out of the house while I snuck in and did my romantic comedy bullshit. I quickly ran out the door and drove home. Later when her mom gave me the signal that they were coming home, I called her and said that I had a surprise for her. The giggles in her voice got me so excited to see her reaction. She walked into the house and sees one red rose and a note right on it. She told me "Mike what is this?!?! OMGOMG is this for Homecoming…" That poor girl got soo excited. But when she opened it, all it said was "Hey Rebecca, thanks for the sandwich today.. It was really tasty, Mike" and at that moment she erupted at me on the phone because the dance was right around the corner and I hadn't asked her yet.

Later that night, I called her and asked her what she was doing. She told me she was just watching TV so I told her to walk upstairs and tell me when she was in the room. She walked in turned on the lights and said, "What the hell Mike what do you want. I was so excited for you to ask me today but you didn't". That is when I told her to turn off the lights. She was so confused, but she did in anyway. The moment she turned off the lights, the entire room shined with glow in the dark stars that could not be seen before because it was too light in the room. Her ceiling was covered from wall to wall and it was as if the entire constellation was right before her eyes. I then told her to go to her bed and to lay down. She did. Then on the phone I said "Rebecca look up." Right over her head were the words "Homecoming?" Made by the glow in the dark stars. Teary eyed, she said "Mike, I hate you... But of course I will go with you"

This relationship was awesome because it was the first time that I was able to show a girl just how much she meant to me. But as cool and awesome as the beginning stages sounded it ended up taking a turn for the worst out of nowhere.

Completely blindsided, one day I get a phone call of her crying. I thought she was hurt so I asked what was wrong.

Turns out she wasn't the one that was hurt, it was me. That call was her telling me that she cheated on me...

My heart was ripped out of my chest. After a full year of doing everything for this girl she ended up being unfaithful. I don't know if you have ever been cheated on, but when you find out it is like this knot in your stomach that you just can't get rid of. You literally have to sit in your own depression wondering why the hell that would happen after everything was working out so good.

But you know what? It was ok. Because this was just the first love of my life. The first love of your life is there so that you can truly appreciate the relationships you have afterwards. It's what makes you stronger. Dude this was my first relationship, so everything from this was just an awesome learning experience. It was because of this experience; the following relationship I had was fucking amazing.

One of the biggest things I learned from this relationship is that in the beginning, I would do all this cute stuff that impressed her, and she would do the same back to me. But it was the moment that we stopped trying to impress each other that led to the downward turn of the relationship. You see relationships are either growing or dying. And if you aren't doing anything to make your relationship stronger with your significant other than it is dying as the automatic alternative to not trying. That is exactly what happened in this relationship. We went from people with a lot of friends, always dressed up nice, and going out... To a poisonous relationship of eating junk food while watching TV alone and avoiding our friends.

This same thing happens to all my friends that initially get into relationships. It starts off great but eventually both sides get lazy and they just slowly lose interest. What is even worse is seeing two people that have no more interest in each other but are STILL together because they are comfortable and too scared to go back out in the real world and be alone.

Was cheating on me her fault? Maybe it was maybe it wasn't, I will never know. But what I do know is instead of blaming her and pointing fingers, I needed to look in the mirror and blame the person that I became at the end of the relationship. Because for every finger you point to blame other people three are pointing back and blaming you. I knew that I was the issue because I lost what initially got her attracted to me in the first place and that was my sense of adventure and craziness.

If you are in a poisonous relationship
Do you know people that are in a relationship simply because they are too scared to face the world alone?
Are you settling in a relationship simply because it is easier than finding someone better that you actually deserve?
Are you with someone that lifts you up or pushes you down?
If they push you down why are you still with them?

If you are in an awesome relationship
Are you doing the little things every day to make sure your relationship grows?
Do you constantly try to impress/surprise your partner?
What can you do today that will make your relationship move forward instead of backward?

Like I said going through this lesson and realizing that I needed to get to work on myself if I wanted to live a good life and have a fulfilling relationship was one of the best lessons I could have ever gotten earlier on in life.

Chapter 21 Enter Love #2

This love was perfect and yet imperfect all at the same time. It is the love you experience with someone whose goals, dreams, and ambitions line up with yours... Someone you can see having a future with... And someone that you can see growing old with... The worst part of this love is that it is destined to fail because the timing is just completely off.

It was the first week of college. My fitness was on point, my confidence was through the roof, and I was super obnoxious. The first week of college is hilarious because everyone is still trying to figure out their place in the world so everyone super shy. Luckily for me I had two childhood friends come with me to Marquette University so we basically owned it in the beginning.

The University assigned us all into small groups to do a quick meeting before we explore the campus, but instead of following the group that I was assigned to I just ended up following my friend Kate (one of the childhood friends) to her group.

We barged into the small group meeting extremely late. And everyone immediately looked at me and gave me the dirtiest look possible. I mean can you blame them? When a 6-foot-tallAsian with a cut off shirt showing off his huge muscles, a tilted hat that screams "I am a gangster", and a half eaten pop-tart walks into a room... I would give that person a dirty look too. But yes, I am the worst at first impressions. Kate quickly sat down so I ended up sitting in the only seat available. I sat down and looked around to see who was around me and immediately as I turn my head to check, this pretty little blonde with the bluest of eyes just begins to stare deep into my soul.

Actually thinking about it in retrospect she was most likely just eyeing the pop-tart I was eating and was just mad jealous that she didn't have one of her own. But man was she pretty. She was wearing these tight blue jeans that showed off her curvy hips, she wore this yellow fitted long sleeve shirt that showed of her tight little waist. Her skin was the perfect sun kissed tan from the long summer days'jet skiing and boating at her grandparents' house in Michigan.

She effortlessly walked through the room with sassiness in her step and with such poise and confidence. And I was like "oh shit... Who the hell is this girl." But of course, whenever I see a pretty girl my brain does this funny thing where it just stops working. I tried to walk up to her and say hi but instead my feet walked me to the Kleenex where I pretended to blow my nose because I was too nervous to say hi. She was probably the prettiest girl I have ever seen and I was completely blowing it. Other than the fact that I had a pop-tart. That was the only thing she ended up noticing about me later on when we spoke about how we met. Well anyway, the small group meeting ended and I didn't even end up getting her name.

In my mind I was like, "FUCKKKK... I literally just blew my chance with the prettiest girl I have ever seen to date."

Even after messing up... I knew that I needed to see her again.

The next day every college freshman decided to go to the beach, which in Milwaukee, Wisconsin, is just a lake with fake sand and dirty Lake Michigan water. Me and my friends end up going there and I just knew that I had to see her. I don't even know her name what the hell. I was on a mission. As we arrive to this "beach" we see a bunch of other college kids awkwardly hanging out and drinking beer.

"Looks like we found the place," My friend Dom said as we arrived. We ended up opening the beers we had and began to toss the football back and forth. What came next was also another one of my dumb ideas in my attempt to talk to a girl. I ended up seeing her out of the corner of my eye playing in the water with her friends. I started to run over to her to awkwardly say hi.But again my brain was doing thatweird thing where it stops working.

I would run closer and closer... Oh crap. She was wearing a bikini... Abort abort...Regroup. That is what my brain made me do as I was trying to approach her. So I circled back around and rethought of a battle plan. I looked at my friend Dom and I said "Listen dude... I am going to go into the water. I want you to throw the ball to me. So I ran into the water and was about 5 feet away from her. I felt like she knew I was there but was way too polite to say anything about my awkwardness and blatant attempt of flirting.

The next 5 seconds were not planned.

My friend ends up throwing the ball to me... And I instead of going for the ball.. End up "accidentally" tackled her into the water. What the hell brain? I wanted you to pretend to bump into her and save her from the football Dom was throwing... Why the hell did you make me tackle her? But regardless, we both plunge into the water. After we both emerged from the depths of the shallow lake water. She looked at me with eyes that nearly could have killed me. But after that intense eye contact. She ended up laughing really loud. In my head I was thinking "Phewww Mike she's laughing... Don't fuck this up now... Quick ask her her name"

"What's your name?"
"Tessa, what's yours?"
"Mike, nice meeting you"

We then hung out for a bit and she asked if I was the douche bag that brought in a pop-tart in the small group meeting the other day...

"Duhhh, of course it was me" and we ended up having a good time and I joked about her having some type of fetish for pop tarts... I saved her in my phone as "Tessa Girl with The pop tart Fetish"

So guys' moral of the story... Whenever you want to talk to someone you like, just make the first interaction the most awkward as possible. It usually ends up working. Just kidding.

So later that day I was playing the guitar trying to make some music with another buddy that was in my dorm building. And I get a text from the Pop Tart Fetish Girl Tessa saying she wanted to hang out. In my mind, I thought holy shit. This girl wants to like make out with me or something so I got super nervous, ended up kicking my roommate out of the room, took a couple shots of this 99 proof alcohol that tasted like bananas to calm the nerves... And as she came in I was like ahhhh getting lucky on the first day of college woot woot!

But I didn't, we just ended up watching Charlie's Angels on Netflix and she declined every single advancement I tried on her. So I ended up going into my cabinet and pulled out a packet of Pop Tarts and we just end up sitting there happily eating our crumbly snack.

After a couple of months of her being the biggest tease known to humankind. We ended up dating. I asked her out to Navy Pier in Chicago. After we rode the huge Ferris wheel and spent stupid amount of money on random stuff that I thought would interest her. She didn't really care because she just wanted to hang out with me. In all honesty I wasn't wanting to be in a relationship, it just happened. We ended up going in a photo booth where it took 3 pictures of us every 3 seconds.

In the first picture you see me and her fighting for the seat and laughing. In the second picture you see me and her looking at each other which is the moment where I asked her if she wanted to be my girlfriend. Then on the last picture you see us kissing after she said yes. We dated for the next several years and it was one of the craziest adventures that I have ever had with a woman.

All our friends said that we were some of the weirdest people they have ever met. We would laugh at our dumb stupid jokes. I think the most awesome thing is that every single day we always tried to impress each other. And every single day, (as lame as it sounds, but screw you for thinking it) we fell more and more in love.

But man was I broke.

I wanted to take her on crazy adventures around the world. I wanted to experience everything out there that there was to experience with her. But the best that I could do was buy a $5 pizza every Tuesday and a cheap bottle of wine. The coolest thing though is she didn't care. She was so supportive and she was always there for me whenever shit in my life would hit the fan.

But as we got older we knew it couldn't last... She was going to leave to Michigan to become a news reporter and I was going into dental school. We knew that this wasn't going to last forever and that we had to go our separate ways. Earlier on the book I also told you that my family and I were going through some financial problems at the time. So that coupled with the idea of separating with one of the most amazing girl in the word made me develop this anger inside of me.

At first I was angry at the situation because I thought it was something I couldn't control. Then I started to get angry at her for no reason. And then we started fighting for no reason. And finally, one of the most perfect relationships that was fit for one of those movies ended up ending because the time was just not right. Life was pulling us in our separate directions wnd I had too much on my plate to worry about helping my family and their finances that I could not give her the love and attention that she deserved. So we split up.

And that is also around the time where I was laying on my floor broke, angry, and depressed. The time where I decided to leave the dental field completely and left school to find a better way.

Have you ever had what seemed to be a perfect relationship?
What prevented you from experiencing all that you could in that relationship?
Was it the lack of time?
Or was it the lack of money?
Was it both?

This is why I focus so deeply on creating time freedom for yourself. So that when you stumble upon an awesome person, you don't have anything stopping you from living the most amazing life possible with that person.

When you have all the time and money in the world, money becomes irrelevant. All you have is pure freedom to express all the dreams, wants, and desires that you have ever wanted with the person that you care about.

Guys don't be like me and let the perfect situation slip out of your fingers. I did and I kick myself every single day for letting something so awesome and so amazing go.

What can you do today to make sure that this doesn't happen to you?
Take action now.

Chapter 22 Enter Love #3

The third love that you will experience is the love that surprises you when you least expect it but it will be the one that lasts a lifetime. Now I am in no rush, I am only 22... But I have done certain things in my life to increase the probability for me to find the perfect woman for me and to make sure that I don't fuck this one up when the time comes.

So as you know, the last relationship talked about in this book ended up horribly. I was broke, I was depressed, the timing was off, and I just lost everything from my girlfriend to my future job as a dentist. Luckily in that same year, I ended up building up a considerably large sized business and have even hired a team of amazing people to help run it for me.

Now the next thing I did was weird but it still follows the laws of the Lazy Man's Guide to Living The Good Life... so please don't judge me when I tell you this. So I took a portion of the profits from the business and used it to go to Vegas for a month where I would learn from a dating coach. I think we wrote it off in our taxes as "sales training" or something. But any who, this was a big aspect of my life that I was lagging on ever since my last relationship ended and I had no idea what to say or even talk to girls.

As you probably know by now, I always end up doing the weirdest thing to get a girl's attention like falling or fake tackling them into water so I needed to find a mentor that had the results that I wanted and to see what he did to get confident to talk with a confident woman.

This was the weirdest month ever. I was able to convince my close friend Roy, who also just suffered a horribly break up to come with me. He bought his ticket the next day.

Even though my business was booming, I still didn't want to suffer lifestyle inflation that was talked about in the wealth pillar section. So I got the small salary that I was paying myself and ended up reserving one whole month at the Hooters Hotel in Las Vegas for $30/day... yep they actually have hotels instead of just making chicken.

The room was dirty, it was dark, and the entire place looked condemned and unused in years, but man were we excited. We both just got out of 3 and 4-year relationships and this was the first time we would learn how to confidently say hi to a girl without the fear of running the other direction when they reject us.

We get a very mysterious email telling us to meet in a random parking lot off of the strip where you will be picked up by a limo and driven to the secret location where this mysterious man named Luke was going to drop some knowledge bombs on how to confidently talk to a woman.

We arrived to the random parking lot and met up with a huge group of dudes all ranging from ages 21 to 55. Everyone looked really confused and was probably wondering the same thing I was on what the hell are we doing in a parking lot.

Then out of nowhere from the desert of Nevada. This huge black limo truck comes over the horizon with tinted black windows so you can't even see inside of it. I honestly didn't know what to expect next. As we all walked into the limo we were greeted with a huge stripper pole right in the middle of the limo. First off... That is a safety hazard. And Second... What the hell did I just get myself into?! I looked over at Roy and I knew that he was thinking the same thing. The limo drives us in all directions almost as if trying to disorientate us so we wouldn't know the exact location of the meeting place for the seminar.

Then suddenly the limo truck stops. And we all wonder what is about to happen next. A bald man from the middle east came into the car door, and with a booming voice, said that we have arrived to the seminar location. He led us through a long hallway leading to the seminar room. I was greeted with half naked women all around me...Woahhh was not expecting that. Apparently the seminar room, was in the same building as the strip club.

I've never been to a strip club in my life before that so I was surprised at all of these women being super forward. I awkwardly sipped on my water through a straw all these girls tried asking for a dance. All I could think about in my mind is "there is no way I can write any of this as a business expense"

My first time was nerve wrecking. I didn't know where to look at so I just looked at my phone as I didn't want to insult the women working. So I awkwardly just sat there waiting for the damn seminar to start.

The middle eastern man with the booming voice then said, "alright guys' seminar is about to begin" and leads us into a secret hallway that connected to a different building that looked like a legit office. It was there did I see seats and a setup that looked like the typical seminar set up.

We waited for about 30 minutes and then all of a sudden a large man with a thick beard, fabio like hair, dressed in all black, with a beer belly walks in and introduces himself as Luke. He apparently is the main instructor that would teach us how to confidently talk to women.

What I can sum up from the 30 days of him dropping knowledge that the only way to get better with confidently talking to women is to throw yourself in more situations where you have to force yourself to think on the spot. It definitely made sense. It's kind of like in business where you fail over and over again and you find out all the ways that DON'T work that you finally found one way that does. With talking to women you just need to get used to that feeling of nervousness you feel whenever going up to her. And the more you just go up and say "Hi" and figure out what you are going to say after the better you will get.

That was a relief. I thought I had to memorize scripts and tricks almost as if I was tricking these girls to like me. But when he told me that I just had to get used to the feeling of nervousness by embracing the situation for what it is instead of what I would like it to be. My confidence with talking to women grew.

Now I am no master pick up dude. If anything I think I got worse. But the biggest thing I learned that helped me with my confidence is to just get used to the chaos and to embrace feeling uncomfortable. The only way to grow in life is to push past your comfort zone. And believe me for those next 30 days I was pushed passed all my limits of what it means to be comfortable. But that is a story for another book.

I used the new found confidence and began to travel the world indefinitely. All while building my business, increasing my health, and finding love.

I would have never been able to do this if I forced myself into a profession that I did not like or have the values that I considered important.

I want freedom from restriction. I didn't want someone telling me what to do. So I created the lifestyle that I wanted instead of living one that was forcibly given to me.

Now even though I have not yet found this third love, and am in no rush because I am so young, I am just grateful that I decided to take action when I needed to, to give me this life that I wanted. So that wherever she is out there in the world, I'll be prepared to live one crazy life with that awesome woman.

What is the person that you would dream of being with?
What is stopping you from getting that person?

Through this entire journey... You cannot convince someone to fall for you. You need to BECOME the person that that person you want is attracted to. And the only way to do that is to be so deep into your mission of focusing on the 4 pillars of the Good Life.

Say you actually took the time to create your dream life?
What would that dream like look like with the person that you want to be with?
Where would you go?
What crazy things would you do?

I want you to start thinking of the craziest, wildest things you would want to experience with your loved one in this short life. And just be grateful that we live in a time where any of this is possible.

Chapter 23 Finding love? ... or getting drunk and lost

Not all my stories end up with me finding my true love... As sappy as it sounds. Some of them are just awesome stories that I think are just awesome to have experienced...

For example, one day I was with my buddy in New York, and we end up going to a bar to which we get near the point of blacking out from all the alcohol. But in my memory, I do recall seeing the most beautiful Spanish girl I have ever seen. She was short and curvy with a sassy personality and I wanted to say hi. So of course, seeing that I learned nothing from the dating instructor, I took 3 more shots and pretended to trip and fall right by her (hey don't judge... It has worked fabulously with my last two girlfriends so why quit what already is proven to work for me?)

Immediately she shoved me off like I was the bubonic plague. But either way, my bouncy personality and awkward sense of humor ended up making her laugh. Her name was Lauren and she was a college student at the time. I asked her more about herself and she told me how she was super into health and was vegan... My heart literally imploded. I told her "Holy shit I tried being a vegan for a week" (in which I was not successful because I believe I am a carnivore at heart) and I really enjoyed her passion when it came to talking about health - which you know is one of the pillars of the good life.

Either way my friend ends up leaving us and it was just me and her at the bar incoherently laughing as we were drunk out of our minds by the end of the night. She tells me about her family and I tell her about mine. She tells me about her goals to finish school and to start her own business and that was a check mark in my book. I was like holy shit this girl is goal orientated AND she wants to create a business. I think I just found a keeper. She calls for an Uber and we say our good byes... Luckily, my phone was dead so I couldn't call an Uber so I had to share hers... Whoops.

We end up driving me home which was at a hotel by the airport. She agreed and the Uber driver drove into that general direction. Then the craziest idea came up in my brain. I asked myself, "Mike, how epic can I make this story?" and I thought hmmm.. It is only 1 am why end the night now? In the back of my mind I thought it would be really cool, almost like a movie, if we just went straight to the airport and flew to a random city somewhere else.

My business was doing well, so I was like heck why not. But I wanted to see if she was down for it and not just some gold digger. So I gave her a test... If she were to buy me a drink at the gas station... I would know that she is an independent woman that doesn't just let guys buy all the things for her. So we had the Uber driver drive us to the gas station. I then asked her if she would buy this chocolate milk for me and she said yes of course. Independent woman test passed! Time to go travel to a random city...

So as we are driving towards my hotel and I asked her if she was adventurous. She said hell yes. I said what was the craziest thing she has done and she asked me the same thing. Turns out, we both didn't do anything super crazy in our life. So we agreed to go to the airport and to figure out what we were going to do from there.

In my drunken haze, I managed to buy two tickets to Miami, Florida. And the plane was boarding in 40 minutes. We stumbled through security and made our way to the other side.
We made the most hilarious conspiracy theory and told everyone we are getting hitched right now and to not tell anyone. Everyone

around us thought it was hilarious. We then passed out on the airplane before it even took off.

I then wake up the next day in a nice hotel right on the beach and she was right next to me... What did we do? Well a gentleman would never tell ;)

This is the level of freedom that you can experience when you have all pillars of your life balanced and when you have the confidence to take all what this beautiful life has to offer. Now if you are married or already have a girlfriend/boyfriend I wouldn't recommend doing my particular example...

But just imagine what would life be like if you had the health, the wealth, the love, and the happiness that you deserve? What is the feeling you would feel knowing that all pillars are in check and constantly growing?
What adventures would you have your online business pay for?
Anything in this world is possible as long as you can perceive it in your mind.

The only thing stopping you is the bullshit story you tell yourself on why you can't have what you want.

Pillar 4: Happiness

Chapter 24 Almost the end

As I am writing this part of the book at the airport I look over to my left and see all my belongings packed up in one backpack. I am going to be traveling around the world indefinitely until I find out more about myself as I face new challenges and adventures alone. Every day will be a new story and every moment will be filled with new adventure. And I am excited to record everything and upload it on the Mike Vestil YouTube channel for all you guys.

But as I am sitting here typing, I realized something that I forgot to really appreciate for a while. For the first time after living this crazy life of mine... I realize, that I am actually happy.

I used to think that buying the nicest cars or the biggest houses were the secret to happiness. I thought that in order to be happy you need to show everyone around you just how happy you are. But no.

What I have come to realize in my short life is that happiness is not about the things you buy, but it's about the experiences that you get to live with the people you care about.

"Life is not measured by the breaths you take, but by the moments that take your breath away" - Anonymous

That is why I committed the next couple of years to only buy what I can carry on my back. And to continue on my journey to living the good life. I believe the only way to achieve happiness in life is two things: To grow, and to give. The moment you find your online business to fund your dream lifestyle I suggest you do the same.

Growing up in Chicago made it so easy to get lost in my self-image. As much as I told myself I didn't care, I would still worry about what people would think about me. I always wanted to keep up with my appearance to the world.

The more success you obtain, the more people believe that you should match that ideal image of what it means to be "rich." But I don't want to be rich in things, I want to be rich in experiences. That is why over the past couple years after building my business I wanted to see just how much I could grow and just how much I could give.

Chapter 25 To grow

Embrace death.

I mean it.

People always ask me if I am afraid to die. Hell yes I am. But I also appreciate it.

"The way I look at it, it's the knowledge that I know I'm going to die that creates the focus I bring to being alive... That creates the urgency of accomplishment and creates the need to express love... Now not later" - Neil De Grasse Tyson

Life is too short to waste even just one day. So how do we find happiness when we know one day we are going to die?

It's to realize that you need to fall in love with the journey of living the good life, not the destination. It is the growth that we experience when working on ourselves and the 4 pillars when we can truly be happy. How about you? Ever accomplished one of your goals? What was more satisfying... The actual moment that you accomplished something you always wanted? Or the journey and the satisfaction you felt growing into the person that deserved what it is you just accomplished?

More simply put. Happiness = To grow.

And as human beings we only have two options. To grow, or to die. There is no in between.

What is going on in your life right now?
Are you growing?
Or are you dying?

At the end of the day no one else can force you on this journey but yourself. So make sure you do everything that you can to grow the 4 pillars, to grow you.

Everyday find ONE THING that you can do to grow in each of the pillars
What is one thing you can do to move closer to your health goals?
What is one thing you can do to move closer to your wealth goals?
What is one thing you can do to move closer to your love goals?

And remember slow progress is STILL PROGRESS. A lot of people come up to me and complain that they do not have the life they want yet only after being in business for a couple days. Are you fucking serious? Just the fact that you committed to getting on the journey puts you further ahead than everyone else just aimlessly getting by. Even though you are not where you WANT TO BE, you are not where you USED TO BE. So take the time right now to appreciate how far it is you have already came.

Chapter 25 To give

"We make a living by what we get. We make a life by what we give." - Winston Churchill

One day I was partying in Vegas back when my business was still growing and unstable. I was so depressed, stressed, and especially worried about if I made the right decision to leave the dental field. I was giving myself negative self-talk, questioning my self-worth, and just pushing myself down into a negative spiral.

Luckily, my cousin Albert called me and asked if I wanted to go to Peru next week for some volunteer thing and nonchalantly mentioned that we would also get to see Machu Picchu. In my mind I was like HELL YES I always wanted to see Machu Picchu. So I bought my tickets the next day and got ready to see some llamas. Little did I know what I actually signed up for…

We arrived to the city of Cuzco and everything was just a whole new world to me. (That may or may not be an Aladdin reference, but the world will never know). The mountains were tall, the air was fresh, and everywhere around me seemed so new and unfamiliar. I was so stuck up that day. I think it was because I thought I was hot shit for having a newly successful business. I tried being cocky about it, but everyone in the volunteer group did not respond well to my ego.

Like I said I am horrible at first impressions...

We all meet up in a random hotel room in the city square for a meeting about the how the entire week was going to work. My cousin and I sat down amongst a bunch of strangers that all turned out to be Mormons. This part was actually pretty interesting because I never crossed paths with a Mormon before, so it was awesome learning about their culture.

They were all such kind and humble people. Looking back, I am so pissed at myself for being such an asshole at a first glance.

As we took our seat the meeting began shortly. I was excited to see what adventures lay ahead for me because I had came just for the llamas and to see Machu Picchu. But these people told me that that was only going to be only one day of this trip and that the rest of the week would be spent fixing up a school.

ARE YOU FUCKING KIDDING ME?! I spent $2000 to get over here and pay for the accommodations just to do manual labor? I was pissed. On top of that my online sales for that day was fluctuating so I was even more mad and stressed as usual. The rest of the day I went back into my hotel room locked myself in the room and just did emails. Everyone asked my cousin why I had a stick up my ass.

The next day we wake up at 6 am and eat breakfast. It was a type of bread that looked like it was a lot but would deflate the moment I put it in my mouth. There was also eggs that came in the smallest of portions. I was starving and the portions here were so small. It angered me even more... and the stick up my ass only got bigger and I got more reactive to my environment.

I ended up downing some special tea that they had to prevent altitude sickness (fun fact the tea leaves they use are the same that can chemically turn into cocaine I think lol but no worries I only drank their tea haha). My cousin, and a bunch of our new random friends, and I got on the bus to go to the school.

As we arrived I was worried if my team was actually doing the work they said they would do, I was worried about if the ads I had set up were converting sales, and I was worried if I was going to reach the goals I had set for that day seeing that I did not have wifi the entire week. In my mind I was freaking out.

As we arrived, this short woman with a large frame, huge curly hair, a snotty attitude, and a napoleon complex told us what are jobs were to be that day. I ended up getting stuck turning over all the soil in a large lot of land so that they would be able to plant a garden. For the next 4 days me and a couple other guys hacked away at the hard soil until that huge field of grass was turned over into soil for the garden.

The work was agonizing. My entire body was sore, my hands were severely callused, and my neck was burnt from the direct contact from the sun. The craziest thing about ending the work, I realized I was happy? What the hell I was worried and stressed out of my mind just days earlier. And this entire time as I was working with these amazing people to help restore this school. I felt like I was being a part of a bigger purpose. I did not think about my "online sales" or the "busyness of my team" the entire time I was working on helping this community. It was the weirdest phenomenon.

What happened next made me almost cry.

After the last day of the long brutal work, I wiped the sweat off my brow and took a big swig of water. Then out of nowhere music starts playing and I was overtaken by a sea of children. There was so many of them I lost count. But as I looked around, I noticed that some of these kids had down syndrome, others had hearing problems, and some couldn't even see... It turned out that the school we were helping to rebuild was for kids with special needs.

That entire day we all put away our tools and just played with the kids. We sang, we played, and we had epic dance battles. As I looked into all these kids eyes, I noticed that they were all happy. And that is when it hit me. I was living a privileged life, I travel the world, I party in Vegas whenever I want to, and I have a business to fuel my dream lifestyle for me. But looking at these kids eyes, I knew that they were happier than I was.

I was so busy stressing on expanding my business and growing that I failed to appreciate how far I have already gotten. I was beating myself up because I was only giving myself the ability to be happy once I achieved a specific monetary goal. But you know what I realized? You will NEVER be happy if you focus on just earning money.

A lot of students always tell me "Mike, I will only be happy when I make $100 a day". No, you won't. You will NEVER be happy if you are waiting to achieve happiness as a goal. Instead of achieving a goal to be happy, you need to happily achieve. And that is what giving back to these kids in that small little village of Peru gave to me.

When you give back to people that are less fortunate than you, people that have no money, have no ability to see or to hear, are homeless, or kids with disabilities... You realize that a lot of these people have nothing, yet they still are happy. And it's because they keep it simple. Happiness is in the moments you experience not the things you buy. Understanding that there are people out there with far less than you, living a life where they can still be happy allowed me to realize to be grateful for everything I have.

What happens when you give a lot? You get so much more in return.

When you give, you experience this overwhelming feeling of gratitude that consumes your body. And if you live your life every single day knowing that you have things to be grateful for, regardless how down or depressed you may feel... You can still live the good life.

"Better to lose count while naming your blessings than to lose your blessings to counting your troubles" - Maltbie Davenport Babcock

No matter how far behind you think you are or how much you think you have NOT yet accomplished...

What are some things that you are grateful for?

What are some people that you are grateful for?
What are some lessons you are grateful for?
What are some challenges that you are grateful for?

And remember whatever hardships you are going through right now are just necessary for you to tell your success story. Because if you didn't go through these hard times then you wouldn't be able to appreciate the good times.

Every day I wake up regardless if business is growing rapidly or slowly. I find little wins that I can be grateful for so I can take the challenges of each and every day head on in a positive state.

I wake up and tell myself how grateful I am for the ability to see, so that I can see the look at my loved ones faces when I get them to smile.

I am thankful for my feet and for the ability to walk when many people out there aren't able to.

I am thankful for the ability to live in a world where as long as I am healthy and alive, I can accomplish all the goals I ever want to accomplish.

We tend to take a lot of the things we have in our life for granted, until it is of course way too late.

Constantly giving back and going on these volunteer trips every now and then is a great reminder to be thankful for everything that I have.

And it doesn't matter if you even have NOTHING because you can still find things to be grateful for. You just need to think. It could be the friends you have, the family you have, or the fact that you woke up today when other people sadly lost their life.

When you fill your body with gratitude, fear cannot exist. It is impossible to feel fear and gratitude at the same time. Which is why you want to get yourself in this state of mind before you begin your day.

And if you are able to give and find more things to be grateful for, then you have found the secret to happiness.
Allow yourself to be happy with the things that you have already had the blessing to experience.

Chapter 26 Your mission now

I know I went through a lot in this book, but I hope the things I have covered stick with you throughout your hardships and your fortune…

Your mission now is to pick ONE THING to take action on today.

What do you commit yourself to doing RIGHT NOW?

Write it down here:

_____

If you ever need a kick in the butt, then you can watch my Mike Vestil YouTube Channel and I can be your accountability partner to make sure you do what you need to do so you can live the life that you deserve.

Who are 3 people that you know this book would help?

Write their names below

1. _____
2. _____
3. _____

I wrote this book to help you. The least you can do is recommend it to your 3 friends so it can help them as well.

And if you are sitting here reading the end *thinking "holy shit that was an abrupt ending and I feel like I have no closure from the story"*

Then PERFECT.

That is because the story hasn't ended yet. And yours has only begun. So instead of just finishing this book and feeling good about yourself, you need to realize that you need to do everything in your power today to get started.

In the meantime you can follow the adventure on social media

YouTube: Mike Vestil
Instagram: mikevestil
Snapchat: mmmmmmmmmmmike (mike with 11 m's)

So you can take a peak on what The Lazy Man's Guide to Living The Good Life really looks like.

Peace out..

Mike Vestil

Made in the USA
San Bernardino, CA
07 August 2018